SUBLIMINAL COMMUNICATION

EMPEROR'S CLOTHES OR PANACEA?

With How to Create Your Own Subliminal Program

by ELDON TAYLOR

JAR

**Just
Another
Reality**
Box 7116
Salt Lake City
Utah 84107

ACKNOWLEDGMENTS
Tony Markham — Cover Art
Mark Latkowski — Statistical Analysis
Charles F. McCusker — Abstract
Roy K Bey, for support and encouragement
without which this book would not have been possible.
Lee Liston, for his tireless efforts
within the Utah prison system.

To Annette, Darlene and Vickie

with special thanks to
Carolyn, Mary Ann, and Norma

TABLE OF CONTENTS

THE AUTHOR

Eldon Taylor has earned doctoral distinction in divinity, pastoral psychology, and metaphysical science. He is the founder of the Institute of Noetic Metaphysics and the creator behind the Mind Mint franchise system. Dr. Taylor is a licensed lie detection examiner and investigator. He is a professional hypnotist specializing in forensic work.

Dr. Taylor's complete biography can be found in a number of Who's Who publications including the *International Who's Who of Intellectuals.*

Dr. Taylor's straightforward, no-nonsense, bottom-line attitude is reflected in *Subliminal Communication: Emperor's Clothes or Panacea?* No punches are pulled—no hype or jargon is added.

A must on anyone's reading list, *Subliminal Communication: Emperor's Clothes or Panacea?* will change the way you do not think about thinking!

INTRODUCTION

The purpose of this work is to make available to every interested person the technology commonly referred to as self-help and self-improvement audio programming, at an affordable price and in a practical and understandable way. Self-help products represent a several-billion-dollar annual business. High-tech aids are almost always accompanied with some form of autosuggestion format.

Thoughts *are* things and definitely predispose, if not create, the realities in our individual lives. The problem, or opportunity, depending upon one's perspective, is that many of these thoughts are rooted deeply in the subconscious mind. We may consciously conclude to change this or that, and yet the change just takes on another disguise for not changing. Sometimes this in itself gives positive feedback to an undefined subconscious reality, such as failure. That is to say, if the subconscious expects us to fail, the failure is certain.

It is also the intent of this work to focus specifically on subliminal technology. Does it work? If so, what is the evidence? How does it work? Are there preferred modalities? Can it create basic changes in personality structure? These and many other questions, implications, and ramifications are treated within the pages that follow. My efforts are not intended to represent the final authority. To the contrary, I view myself as an interested investigator and not a "hard scientist." The evidence, however, suggests the need and opportunity for a variety of interesting research projects. Subliminal technology works! The questions now should treat the variety of modalities, subject matter, length of exposure, "best-time-use" approaches, follow-up studies, etc.

In beginning this work, a decision had to be made regarding the technical level of communication desired. It was decided to choose a middle path; consequently, if the interest of the reader is at either the "see Spot run" level or toward technical orientation to, say, the frequency form of electro-magnetic smog perceived at a subliminal or physiological level which may give rise to mutations of the DNA molecule, then the material that follows will be disappointing.

In our society we are exposed daily to some form of subliminal communication, and our only defense is an informed level of understanding. To aid in this understanding is the principle objective of what follows.

CHAPTER 1

HISTORY

Subliminal communication is much older than one might think. As far back as the turn of the century, the concept of the subliminal mind was one of controversy. Some behavioral scientists were utilizing a technique referred to as "whisper" technology in clinical sessions with patients. The idea was, and still is, very simple. If the conscious mind listens to a statement, for the most part it has the prerogative to accept, reject, or modify the statement. For instance, if the conscious mind is told that one feels good, it may argue with the statement. However, the subconscious does not have the same discriminate ability. If the subconscious accepts that one feels good, one feels good!

In 1894, W. R. Dunham, M.D., wrote an interesting commentary on the subliminal mind and subliminal communication that nearly one hundred years later will still read to some as though it were science fiction. Following is an excerpt from Dunham's interesting work *The Science of Vital Force.*

> Ordinary methods of expressing intelligence will be considered as a supraliminal consciousness; while the phrase "subliminal consciousness" is recognized as most appropriate in representation of that more obscure function of mind property and intellectual ability.
>
> The supraliminal consciousness—above the horizon, and within the limit of recognition—constitutes the ordinary voluntary ability of mental function. It is a property or function of mental ability, which no one individual mind can measure, and of greater dimensions than its own circumference; while the boundaries of this function will ever remain undetermined. Not only has this life property the ability to exercise its function in relation to all the external affairs of the universe; but it may operate directly the ultimate vital property, contractility, and indirectly guide, to a limited degree, the vital property, instinct.

There is implied in this vital property, sensibility, an ability to originate ideas and to experience emotions of grief, joy, hope, reverence, and to exercise reason and develop a comprehension of those operative principles of Nature which give variety to the visible universe. The special application we are to make of this function and division, as applicable to our subject, will be largely to illustrate its existence in distinction from other ultimate vital properties, and its co-operation in association with other life properties. Sleep is implied in a complete temporary suspension of the active property, sensibility—a condition from which we may be awakened in various ways, and frequently by the vital property of the individual sensation.

In adopting a name for the obscure division of this mind property, the most advanced thinkers have coined the phrase "subliminal consciousness" as best expressive of an intelligence manifested unlike the ordinary consciousness—an intelligence uprising, as we might say, from a submerged strata of individual personality. And it has been asked, "Is there some pattern in the very fabric of our nature which begins to show when we scratch the glaze off the stuff?" It may be impossible to define where supraliminal consciousness leaves off, and subliminal intelligence begins; but such, at least, is not our purpose. We only desire to call attention to this department in order to illustrate that there is an obscure feature of human intellectual personality of continued increasing complexity—a kind of intelligence emanating from our obscure selves, of mysterious operation, not easy of comprehension, and for purposes not wholly recognized.

We can no better illustrate this department than by mentioning some of the operations thus executed. What is called "automatic writing" consists of a written intelligence from some source, of whose nature and purport the writer's conscious intelligence may have no knowledge, and which is sometimes called "trance writing." The operation implied in a genuine "trance" is an illustration of the exercise of a faculty of subliminal consciousness. This singular ability may be exercised in the dark in such feats as landscape and portrait painting.

This sub-state called "subliminal consciousness" belongs to and is a part of the nature of every individual, existing to a more or less degree; and it is capable of being brought to the surface by a system of cultivation. It is not a consciousness which has been acquired through the culture of supraliminal abilities, but a kind of innate consciousness which may acquire intelligence by an entirely different method—a consciousness which may possess wonderful faculties even in persons whose ordinary intelligence may be mediocre and even below par, illustrated frequently in mathematical and musical "freaks," so called. It is not unreasonable to suppose that much of the most brilliant genius of historic mention may have been found in persons capable of drawing on this quality of highly endowed natural ability. For this subliminal consciousness, with some individuals, has the ability of silent communication. In other words, the subliminal consciousness of A may learn of the subliminal consciousness of B what might be known by his supraliminal consciousness. Thus A may learn the thought and facts known only to B, which is often accomplished in test proceedings, and is called "telepathy." The supraliminal mind may imagine itself, and really be, on any part of the globe, while the subliminal may have even a greater ability: it may describe accurately the things seen; it may enter the residence of persons miles away, and describe all there is in the room as correctly, in many instances, as an individual presence might accomplish. Such feats are called "clairvoyance"; and clairvoyance consists in a temporary suspension of the supraliminal mind, and the exercise of the subliminal abilities. Hypnotism consists in a temporary suspension of the supraliminal faculties of A, while the supraliminal consciousness of B becomes operative with both the thought and voluntary mechanism of A; and when complete, the voluntary mind of B, with the good subject, may cause hypnotic A to speak the thought of B, while A is not conscious of thus doing.

But how is this done? The explanation, we fear, would be as difficult as to explain how we think.

In the exercise of the subliminal faculties it is possible that A may speak or write a foreign language wholly unknown to A in his normal condition, it being the native language of B. Thus A may know through the subliminal consciousness of B the language which B speaks, and may write a message in that language relative to which B has knowledge, while A may have no knowledge of the language or of the incident mentioned in the message. When a child or an untutored individual goes into a trance, uses the subliminal faculties, and writes in a language unknown to his normal consciousness, the inference is often accepted that the "spirit" of some distinguished dead person is using this particular organism to communicate with the living. Such incidents, however, are telepathic operations, constituting a subliminal exchange of intelligence. The child's subliminal consciousness is in telepathic communication with the same faculty of one who speaks such language.

No well-informed person will deny the existence of the alleged subliminal consciousness. Neither is it intellectually prudent to circumscribe the limits and abilities of such division of intellectual function in living human individuality. That agency which has been recognized and given the name of "psychic force" is a factor of the subliminal consciousness. This comparative recent discovery of an agency, frequently presented unconsciously through the living human organism, is receiving much attention from the most

advanced minds in civilized countries; and to mention
the many singular and varied presentations of this
agency would require more space than we can give to
this interesting department.

Most people are aware of what brought subliminal out of the
closet, but in the interest of continuity let us review the more
recent history.

In the 1950s, a New Jersey theater owner reported flashing
refreshment subliminals during the showing of the movie
Picnic. According to claims, flashing the words "Drink Coca-
Cola" over Kim Novak's face resulted in a 58 percent increase in
Coca-Cola sales over a six-week period.

Vance Packard's work *Hidden Persuaders* appeared in 1957
and although discredited by many, found itself on the required
reading list for many high schools by the late sixties. Packard
quoted from the *London Sunday Times* an account of a New
Jersey theater where ice cream ads were flashed onto the screen
during a movie showing. That also resulted in an otherwise
unaccountable increase in ice cream sales. The *Times* referred to
this technology as "subthreshold effects."

Whether labeled as "subthreshold" or "subliminal," the
nature of the communication is such that the conscious mind
does not perceive it and, in many instances, could not perceive it.
(For a more detailed discussion of semantics and definitions, see
Chapter 3 regarding legislation attempts.)

Packard's work warned of psychologists turned merchan-
disers and of the resulting psychoseduction of the American
consumer. From belief systems to product identification,
Packard presented a case for persuasion through the art and
science of motivational analysis, feedback, and psychological
manipulation. *Hidden Persuaders* was the first open attempt to
inform the general public of a potentially Orwellian means to
enslave the mind and to do so surreptitiously.

Since the New Jersey theater story, headline stories have
appeared in nearly all major publications denying reports of
subliminal technology use. The subject matter of these stories
ranges from sports motivation to the reduction of pilferage.

By 1980, the McDonagh Medical Clinic in Gladstone, Missouri, had installed a subliminal processor to mix spoken words at an imperceptible level with music to relax patients. The clinic reported a decrease in patient anxiety levels, attested to by the absence of fainting. When the subliminal message was removed, patients began fainting again.

How far back the use of subliminal communication reaches and in what guises it is affecting each of us today makes interesting conjecture. It is asserted that Alfred Hitchcock inserted subliminal words such as *blood*, *knife*, and *murder* in the first release of the movie *Psycho* for the purpose of heightening fear in the audience.

So far as this author can ascertain, the earliest audio use of subthreshold communication (aside from the whisper therapy alluded to earlier) was employed by Lozanov in Bulgaria and used to enhance learning abilities in the areas of language and mathematics. Lozanov's technique put much more emphasis on other aspects of what has become known as suggestopedia, however, than it did on the use of subliminals.

Then along came the Becker "black box." Dr. Becker, a former professor at Tulane University, patented a "little black box" that mixed spoken words with Muzak at levels subaudible to the conscious mind. (For more on the Becker process, see Chapter 6 regarding the process of audiosubliminal creation.) Becker's box was initially tested in department stores where messages such as "I am honest" and "I will not steal" were credited with dramatic reductions in inventory shrinkages.

Wilson Brian Key, who has been charged by critics with having a "dirty mind" and thereby reading filth into what Key charges are sexually exploitive ads, illustrates in his work *Clam Plate Orgy* subliminal and supraliminal content in advertising and art going back as far as the Sistine Chapel (*supraliminal* referring to consciously unnoticed, *subliminal* to not consciously perceivable).

One individual this author has spoken with was personally involved in back-masking (a technique generally used to combine subliminal audio tracks with music) messages related to drugs and satanic worship for various rock groups in the early seventies. (See Chapter 6 for details.) According to this person, he stopped doing this when the messages became observable in fans' behavior. The groups, including such well-known ones as KISS, reportedly came up with the idea from some old Eastern literature as yet unidentified.

However far back subliminals were used and at whatever level of activity they are currently existing, it is nearly impossible to imagine an individual in today's population that has not been exposed to subliminal persuasion techniques of one kind or another. How *much* subliminal massaging we are all products of is much more relevant than the question, Have we been subliminally manipulated? For that matter, I would consider it a fair question, after you examine the cover to this book closely, to ask yourself whether or not the word *sex* embcd had anything to do with your acquisition of this book. (See drawing in appendices.)

CHAPTER 2

MECHANICS

Many times I have been asked to explain how a sexual subliminal and/or a horror subliminal can sell a product for an advertiser. I always begin my answer by referring the questioner (as I do you now) to Professor Key's work *Subliminal Seduction*. Key spends a great deal of effort explaining the various psychological mechanisms that make erotic, violent, and generally consciously disgusting material profitable to ad makers. Perhaps most important among them is the repression mechanism. Simply stated, and unbelievable as you may find this, the repression mechanism functions so that one sees only what he wants to see. Now, this is an oversimplification but worth repeating: One sees what he wants to see and fails to see often explicit content that is prohibited by one's own beliefs and expectations.

For example, once while attempting to explain this process to a group of inmates at the Utah State Prison, I passed among the inmate audience a *Playboy* subscription advertisement that appeared in *Subliminal Seduction*. The advertisement portrays a beautiful naked blonde female with a Christmas wreath. Written in the center of the wreath is the statement, "Give him ideas for Christmas." The wreath appears to be made up of walnuts. On close inspection, however, the wreath clearly pictures penis heads and vaginas.

The inmate audience, like the readers of *Playboy*, were consciously unaware of the sexual communication that occurred at a subconscious level, even when instructed to examine the advertisement for such content.

It could be argued that at least two reasons are behind this type of ad. The most obvious is that the subliminal increases the length of time one looks at an advertisement. The second reason is a little more complicated and essentially consists of two parts. The first relates to recall or product identification at point of purchase and the other to some nonconscious excitability that has been linked subliminally to the product.

Thus, perceptual defense mechanisms ranging from repression to sublimination serve as lenses to protect against perceptual damage. It might be valuable to review the basic perceptual defense mechanisms.

1. *Denial.* As implied by its name, this mechanism is simply one of denying. Often the denial occurs through projection, that is, projecting blame or fault on another.

2. *Fantasy formation.* This major mechanism creates a perceived reality out of fantasy. If motives cannot be satisfied in the objective external world, they may become a reality in a dream world. Some psychologists suggest that the appeal for much of our entertainment is satisfaction oriented to our fantasies for adventure, affection, and security, perhaps not so vividly experienced otherwise.

3. *Introjection.* Introjection places blame on oneself. This self-directed blame or punishment defends against disappointment or disillusionment in another. For example, a child feels unworthy of the parent's attention because the parent pays no attention to the child.

4. *Isolation.* This involves the avoidance of connecting associations to related ideas that produce anxiety. One set of data is isolated from an associated set: birth is isolated from death, war from mourning, nuclear arsenals from murderous horror, and so forth.

5. *Projection.* Simply stated, this mechanism allows one to project blame on another.

6. *Regression.* This mechanism is common during serious illness. Essentially, one regresses to an earlier age, usually as a dependent, where he felt safe and comfortable. The individual usually returns to an earlier stage of development where someone else assumed responsibility and where fewer, simpler, and more primitive goals existed.

7. *Repression.* Generally this is a process that censors or prohibits memories, associations, and adjustments from conscious awareness. Like an invisible filter, this mechanism prevents the conscious mind from "seeing" painful memories and/or "stymied" motives. Personal experiences ranging from embarrassment to cruelty are often subject to the lense of repression.

8. *Sublimination*. This is the redirection of basic drive mechanisms. Sublimination is simply the substitution of acceptable behavior to satisfy basic motives that might be met equally well in a primitive sense by some form of social behavior. For example, basic aggression motives are often met by sports activities. The process of sublimination is to find avenues in which basic motives may be satisfied in a manner acceptable to the individual and society.

In addition, there are a number of miscellaneous escapes and defenses that some theorists consider as contributing to the basic perceptual defenses mentioned above, all for the purpose of showing each of us only what we want to see about ourselves and about the world around us.

It should be noted also that there can be many mechanisms functioning at one time; in that case, the boundaries overlap, making it difficult to differentiate between the mechanisms.

Repeated experiments have adequately demonstrated that the conscious mechanism is not a necessary part of information processing. In fact, the unconscious can and quite frequently does operate without, or at least unknown to, the conscious mechanism.

Where preconscious predisposition is concerned, Benjamin Libet of the University of California believes that conscious intention only facilitates or inhibits action initiated by the preconscious process. In fact, according to the *Brain-Mind Bulletin*'s report on Libet's work, correlates between EEG patterns and conscious experience reveal that 350 milliseconds before the subjective experience of, say, wanting to move, distinct activity in brain-wave patterns occurs. Libet views this model as understanding choice. One chooses to act or not. He does not necessarily choose what to act upon.

It is noteworthy that where brain wave activity is concerned, research has confirmed an increase in pattern activity on test subjects who listened to music containing a subliminal message compared to the effect of listening to the same music without the hidden messages. Without conscious awareness, the brain appeared to be processing and otherwise responding to unconscious stimuli.

Dr. Poetzle is credited with contributing one of the first scientifically meaningful findings regarding subliminal communication. Poetzle, working with dream content, discovered that material perceived consciously does not appear in dreams. Information and stimuli appearing in dreams is apparently drawn from unconsciously perceived stimuli prior to the dream. Poetzle therefore concluded that dream content is primarily constructed from subliminally perceived material. Poetzle further demonstrated that a conscious association could stimulate a subliminal percept even years after the percept occurred.

The use of phraseology such as *subliminal perception* is awkward, since the terms are mutually exclusive. However, in this sense, the meaning of perception is being stretched to include any level of perception—conscious or unconscious. Research clearly shows that somehow information is processed from stimuli received but not consciously perceived. It is in this sense that stretching the literal use of the word *perception* is necessitated, since there is a lack of adequate terminology.

Data assembled by psychologists and neurologists strongly support the notion that all sensory input is from at least two levels of perception—conscious and unconscious. And more than one notable thinker is of the opinion that no significant belief originates on the basis of data consciously perceived.

From Poetzle's work in the early 1900s to now, subliminal perception has been tested and retested. The results are conclusive. Human activity can be affected by subliminally perceived material in at least eight areas: conscious perception, dreams, drives, emotions, memory, perceptual defenses, value norm anchor points, and verbal behavior.

The purpose here is not a treatise on psychological functions or the nature of consciousness itself. There are volumes by prominent authorities on those subjects. The purpose here is a straightforward, simplified account designed to demonstrate how subliminal processing has been and is accomplished. Despite the possible "Missourian" mentality of "show me" the emperor is wearing clothes. Subliminal communication is real!

During numerous radio talk shows that I have appeared on, I have often been asked, "Do you really believe this stuff?" The answer is absolutely! As to the actual mental mechanics, that is subject to theory and controversy. Much work is going on right now in the various areas and interfaces of behavioral science to produce a better understanding of how the unseen, unheard, unconscious influences are perceived and integrated into consciousness.

The question is not whether but how. Like gravity, electricity, or consciousness itself, our explanations are often, at best, observation points of seen influences interpreted as theories on unseen reality.

CHAPTER 3

THE LAW AND SUBLIMINALS

Most people are surprised to learn that there are no laws regulating subliminal communication. There is no protection from subliminal manipulation, or legal appeal other than the remote possibility of civil remedy.

If it were not unconscionable that nothing has ever been written into law to prohibit subliminal exploitation, it would be amusing. The public reaction of the late fifties and early sixties ended where it began. What was considered by *Newsday* as "the most alarming invention since the atomic bomb" has been shuffled away to "dirty mind" arguments and ghosts that go bump in the night. Those who did not think laws actually had been placed on the books were made to believe that what you could not hear could not hurt you. What you could not see, you didn't see, because it was not there.

In numerous interviews and interactions with the public, I was continually astounded by the number of people who had simply relegated subliminals either to category one: They don't work, they're like the emperor's clothes in the fairytale, call it placebo or call it pretend; or category two: They're against the law.

Although several states and even the United States Senate introduced legislation to prohibit subliminals in public communication media, no legislation was ever enacted.

In 1986, Representative Francis Merrill of the Utah Legislature initiated legislation, this time to prohibit subliminal communication without informed consent. Since this is my home state and the residence of our corporate offices for the Mind Mint stores, and since the Mind Mint specializes in high-tech products for self-help and self-improvement, including over four hundred subliminal titles from several different manufacturers, and since we had hands-on experience resulting from the sale of tens of thousands of tapes and were involved in subliminal research with the Utah State Prison, we became active sponsors of the legislation.

The intent of the proposed legislation, remember, was to prohibit subliminal exposure without informed consent. In other words, just as restaurants years ago posted notices regarding microwave use, a retailer using antitheft subliminals, for example, would be required to inform those who might hear the tapes. Obviously, heavy-metal musical groups using subliminals also would be required to display appropriate notices as would any and all users of subliminal communication.

There were three bills in all, known as H.B. 106, 107, and 108. The exact originally proposed house bills were as follows:

Legislative General Counsel
Approved for Filing: DAT
Date: 12/13/85; 11:44 AM
(Subliminal Communication as Invasion of Privacy)
1986
General Session
H.B. 106   By Frances Hatch Merrill
We oppose surreptitious manipulation for purposes of exploitation.

An act relating to the judicial code; designating subliminal communication without notification as an invasion of privacy; providing remedies; defining terms; and providing a severability clause.

This act affects sections of Utah Code Annotated 1953 as follows:

Enacts:

Chapter 17, Title 78, Utah Code Annotated 1953

Be it enacted by the Legislature of the state of Utah:

Section 1. Chapter 17, Title 78, Utah Code Annotated 1953, is enacted to read:

78-17-1. As used in this chapter, "subliminally embedded communication" means any device or technique that is intentionally used to convey or attempt to convey a message to a person by means of images, writing, or sounds which are not consciously perceivable.

78-17-2. It is an invasion of privacy for any person in this state to convey or cause to be conveyed to any individual any communication which the person knows or should know contains a subliminally embedded communication, unless the person:

(1) makes or causes to be made a notification, in the manner required by Section 78-17-3, of the existence of the subliminally embedded communication; and

(2) provides to the individual, on request, a written description of the content of the subliminally embedded communication.

78-17-3. The notification required by Section 78-17-2 shall:

(1) be reasonably calculated to notify persons to whom the subliminally embedded communication may be transmitted of the existence of the subliminally embedded communication;

(2) include a notification of the availability of a written description of the content of the subliminally embedded communication and of the name and address of the person conveying it or causing it to be conveyed, for use by individuals to whom the communication is conveyed in obtaining the written description;

(3) (a) be made in conspicuously placed and easily legible type, if the communication is intended to be seen; or

(b) be made in a clearly audible manner immediately prior to the communication being made, if the communication is intended to be heard; and

(4) in addition to the requirements of Subsection (3), be made in conspicuously placed and easily legible type on the face of any label or packaging of the medium containing the communication, whether the communication is intended to be seen or heard.

78-17-4. Any individual whose privacy has been invaded as a result of an act described in this chapter, or the state of Utah, may maintain an action to enjoin the continuance of the subliminally embedded communication until the person conveying the communication or causing it to be conveyed makes or causes to be made the notification described in Section 78-17-2 and provides a written description of the content of the subliminally embedded communication to any person requesting it. Actual damages need not be alleged or proved to support the injunction.

78-17-5. In addition to or in lieu of the remedy provided in Section 78-17-3, an individual whose privacy has been invaded as a result of an act described in this chapter may maintain an action against the person who conveyed the communication or caused it to be conveyed for the recovery of three times his actual damages, for punitive damages, and for costs of suit, including reasonable attorney's fees.

Section 2. If any provision of this act, or the application of any provision to any person or circumstance, is held invalid, the remainder of this act is given effect without the invalid provision or application.

Legislative General Counsel
Approved for Filing: DAT
Date: 12/13/85; 11:41 AM
(Subliminal Communication As Unfair Competition)
1986
General Session
H.B. 107   By Frances Hatch Merrill

An act relating to commerce and trade; amending the unfair practices act to include subliminal communication without notification as unfair competition; defining terms; and providing a severability clause.

This act affects sections of Utah Code Annotated 1953 as follows:

Enacts:

13-5-3.1, Utah Code Annotated 1953

Be it enacted by the Legislature of the state of Utah:

Section 1. Section 13-5-3.1, Utah Code Annotated 1953, is enacted to read:

13-5-3.1. (1) As used in this section, "subliminally embedded communication" means any device or technique that is intentionally used to convey or attempt to convey a message to a person by means of images, writing, or sounds which are not consciously perceived.

(2) It is an unfair method of competition in commerce or trade for any person in this state to convey or cause to be conveyed to the public a communication intended to result in monetary gain which the person knows or should know contains a subliminally embedded communication, or to manufacture, distribute, or sell in this state any printed, audio, or visual medium which the person knows or should know contains a subliminally embedded communication, unless the person:

(a) makes or causes to be made a notification, in the manner required by Subsection (3), of the existence of the subliminally embedded communication; and

(b) provides to any person, on request, a written description of the content of the subliminally embedded communication.

(3) The notification required by Subsection (2) (a) shall:

(a) be reasonably calculated to notify persons to whom the subliminally embedded communication may be transmitted of the existence of the subliminally embedded communication;

(b) include a notification of the availability of a written description of the content of the subliminally embedded communication and of the name and address of the person conveying it or causing it to be conveyed, for use by persons to whom the communication is conveyed in obtaining the written description;

(c) (i) be made in conspicuously placed and easily legible type, if the communication is intended to be seen; or

(ii) be made in a clearly audible manner immediately prior to the communication being made, if the communication is intended to be heard; and

(d) in addition to the requirements of Subsection (2)(c), be made in conspicuously placed and easily legible type on the face of any label or packaging of the medium containing the communication, whether the communication is intended to be seen or heard.

Section 2. If any provision of this act, or the application of any provision to any person or circumstance, is held invalid, the remainder of this act is given effect without the invalid provision or application.

Legislative General Counsel
Approved for Filing: DAT
Date: 12/13/85; 11:30 AM
(Subliminal Communication Cause of Action)
1986
General Session
H.B. 108   By Frances Hatch Merrill

An act relating to the judicial code; creating a civil cause of action for injury or death caused by subliminal communication; defining terms; and providing a severability clause.

This act affects sections of Utah Code Annotated 1953 as follows:

Enacts:

78-11-7.5, Utah Code Annotated 1953

Be it enacted by the Legislature of the state of Utah:

Section 1. Section 78-11-7.5, Utah Code Annotated 1953, is enacted to read:

78-11-7.5. (1) An action for damages resulting from injury or death of a person may be maintained by the person or, as permitted by Sections 78-11-6 and 78-11-7, his parent, guardian, heirs, or personal representative, against a person who knowingly communicated or caused to be communicated a subliminally embedded communication which proximately resulted in the injury or death.

(2) As used in this section, "subliminally embedded communication" means any device or technique that is intentionally used to convey or attempt to convey a message to a person by means of images, writing, or sounds which are not consciously perceived.

Section 2. If any provision of this act, or the application of any provision to any person or circumstance, is held invalid, the remainder of this act is given effect without the invalid provision or application.

As has been the case with past attempts at legislation to regulate subliminals, the proposed Utah legislation met with much opposition.

The same week the House committee reviewed Representative Merrill's legislation, the *Wall Street Journal* reported that Uncle Sam was using "Mom" messages to calm workers' nerves. Several studies were made available to the committee demonstrating clearly the efficacy of subliminal technology.

The first day of the committee's deliberation, Barbara Levy, speaking on behalf of the American Association of Advertising Agencies, equated subliminals with ink blot tests, flatly claiming that people can find anything in them. Levy stated, "Subliminal advertising is a myth perpetuated by a few confused consumers."

Terry Jessop, who suggested the bills to Representative Merrill, said, "Ninety-nine percent of all ad agencies are totally ethical.... The basic issue is the right of privacy. A person has a right to his own mind." Jessop is the founder and head of an organization known as the National Institute of Subliminal Research.

Representative Merrill stated that she was concerned about brainwashing.

Chief among the opponents to the legislation was Virgil Hayes, identified as president of the Rocky Mountain Hypnotists Examining Council. Hayes argued that the bills were ambiguous.

At my invitation, the argument was taken to the airwaves for public interaction. The local talk radio station, KTKK, and its evening host, Jim Kirkwood, agreed to a two-hour open discussion.

Joining Mr. Kirkwood and myself were Representative Merrill, Mr. Jessop, and Mr. Hayes. The highlights of the program are quoted from a transcript of the broadcast:

Taylor: I understand the intent of this legislation is to eliminate willful exploitation of the public via subliminal technology.

Jessop: That's correct, Eldon.

Taylor: The Mind Mint thoroughly supports that. Not to support it is un-American. Virgil, you correct me if I get it wrong, but in reviewing the bills myself, I have some problems because the language is rather ambiguous and by definition perhaps could tie the hands of our behavioral scientists, our self-help community, and for that matter maybe even the conversations a mom might have with her child. This is where you are coming from, is that right?

Hayes: I believe that could possibly be the interpretation— as vague as the interpretation is, and I think that's what we're here to address tonight, Eldon. So I think that it might be appropriate if we were to have a partial reading of the bills so that the public might have more of an idea what the bill actually states.

Jessop: Basically we have three bills. H.B. 106 is primarily discussing the use of subliminal communication as an invasion of privacy. It is our contention that an individual has the right to be subjected to whatever they want to be subjected to as long as they have prior notification that they are going to be subjected to this. That's one of the reasons why we believe that it will be found constitutional is because we are not trying to outlaw all subliminals. What the state would be able to do is regulate, with prior notification, any use of subliminals, whether that is done through a professional hypnotherapist, whether it is done in the recording industry, advertising industry, grocery stores, or whatever. Basically, if you go into a doctor's office, you say, "Doctor, I'm sick; I need some help." The doctor would then perhaps administer a prescription or other things that he felt were reasonable. Usually the patient does not say, "Hey, would you tell me what this particular prescription has to do with the healing process?" And so, usually we just let the doctor do whatever he wants to do.

What we would like is, that if a person is going to be subjected to subliminal messages, that is fine as long as the person is aware that they are going to be subjected to subliminal messages. We are definitely aware that there are positive uses of subliminal messages. For example, to help a person lose weight, stop smoking, perhaps to modify deviant sexual behavior, cut down shoplifting, there are positive uses of subliminals; not all subliminal uses are of a negative nature.

Kirkwood: Yes, I even own one. It is the 23rd Psalm subliminal and I listen to it as I drive around.

Jessop: ... positive mental attitude, so many things. We have no conflict with Mr. Hayes or with anyone else interested in being able to use subliminals, provided the individual is aware that they are in a contractual basis, that they are actually receiving subliminals, and that they have the opportunity to receive a transcript of these additionally encoded messages.

Kirkwood: So if that [subliminal message] should be in a cassette or record, it should be on the jacket or something like that?

Jessop: At least notification that there is a subliminal message inside and then a place where they can contact the producers of that particular subliminal message.

Taylor: That is the intent of 106 and 107?

Jessop: Yes.

Taylor: Now, how about 108?

Kirkwood: Starting with those is there any objection to that from either one of you?

Hayes: Well I'd like to start out by saying we are not here as the American Council to be in defense of subliminal signals or subliminal advertising or exploitation. However, we are opposed to H.B. 106, as the intent of the author is substantially different than the writing of 106, in my interpretation. The proposal of 106 is incredibly vague, not specific to the areas of actual concern. We believe that this proposal is not only unenforceable but does not even remotely address the specific problem areas. Now, we do agree with the legislative attorney that this bill could possibly deny freedom of speech as well as freedom of press, and possibly as well to think in ways that are most appropriate to the individual without having legislation. We also believe that 106 should be dismissed or rewritten to meet the specific cause of concern as quickly as possible. We also believe that this bill is unconstitutional and we cannot protect the public from reality; however, what we can do is train the public and educate the public to respond to reality. We believe that education, not legislation is the answer. We also believe that H.B. 106 will create far more problems than it would eliminate. We believe that far more input from those who are experts in the field of communication is necessary to assist in rewriting this proposed bill towards the specific purposes and intent. And we are in agreement as to the intent of H.B. 106. However, in our opinion, as written, it is nonspecific, nondirectional and does not even address the specific issues, and we are on record as opposing H.B. 106 for that reason.

Kirkwood: Okay, now ... so far the intent of the bill is to require notification that there is a subliminal like on a tape or record, radio, and TV. I guess those would be. . . .Of course you couldn't regulate radio and television, could you?

Jessop: Yes, if it is created ... if the advertisements are created within the state and broadcast within the state, yes.

Kirkwood: Is there any problem with that?

Hayes: Well, actually the writing of the bill in itself and the reason we are opposed is because definition in effect covers any and all communication between any and all individuals, i.e., sounds through verbal content and/or nonverbal facial expressions, body positions, style of clothes, hair styles, images, love letters, writing newspapers, books, and will prohibit any of these mediums without making the communicator by law a psychic. So that they may become aware of the subliminally transmitted messages as received by the communicatee.

Kirkwood: Where does that say that in there?

Hayes: In the definition, right?... Let me borrow the bill...Right there, and I want to read that to you.

Kirkwood: Yes, the specific areas now.

Hayes: That's why we needed to read that.... The definition as used in this chapter... "subliminally embedded communication means any device or technique that is intentionally used to convey or sage attempts to convey a mesto a person by means of images, writings, or sounds which are not consciously perceived." And as we have agreed, as most communicators have agreed, that a vast majority of any and all communication is of a subliminal nature, now this could be something even as simple as a baby crying in the middle of the night at 2:00 a.m. to wake mom up. . . .

Kirkwood: The bill says intentionally though.

Hayes: The intentionally. Intentionally means anytime we communicate with an individual.

Kirkwood: Intentionally... does it say intentionally to use subliminal...?

Hayes: To convey or attempt to convey a message to a person by means, images, writings, or sounds which are not consciously perceived, and the fact is the vast majority of communication, whether it's me presenting myself to you on the street socially, has subliminal implications and I think that these need to be cleaned up and addressed so that it doesn't restrict any and all communicators to hang out a sign each time they make a statement to someone such as have a nice day, for example, because of the subliminal implications behind that statement. If a person is having a good day, they might have that amplified; if they're having a bad day, they might take the opposite approach, the reversal effect, and these things are subconscious functions, subliminal functions.

Kirkwood: Terry, you are the director of the National Institute of Subliminal Research; what does that mean?

Jessop: Basically, what our organization is interested in doing is monitoring the use of possibly sexual or satanical subliminals as they're used in magazines, newspapers, television, motion pictures across the United States. People, members of our organization and those who are not, make it possible for us to receive copies or notification of those particular messages which they feel perhaps are documented sources. Basically, where we are coming from is we feel that this is perhaps an extreme interpretation. As we have met with some very responsible lawyers, we have felt that this is not that case; however, I don't feel like it is such a personal thing that I would feel offended if some of the terminology were changed, but as we have been able to speak with the attorneys and as I have had a chance to go through and look at the legislation, I believe it is very responsible, very reasonable, and that's basically where I am coming from.

Hayes: Well, the legislative attorney himself in his report as to the intent of this, 106, 107, and 108, made the statement that it may be challenged on the basis of the federal First Amendment and state constitutional rights to freedom of speech and press and in this particular situation I believe that it would not only do that but it would restrict that freedom of speech as well as press. So, when the term *responsible attorney* has been made I think that this comes from the legislative attorney and I don't know of anyone more responsible in the state.

Taylor: Mr. Taggert, if I am correct, is quoted in today's

newspapers as stating, Virgil, that "juries will decide what is a subliminal message." And, he added, it's a problem of proof, but the law is there to say there is a probable cause of action for, so the entire interpretation if I am understanding this correctly, the entire interpretation of what constitutes a subliminal is something that Taggert is saying a jury would decide.

Hayes: Well, in that particular case, getting back to the subliminal contents. To begin with, as we both know in our particular professions, people can see, hear, and feel what they want to in response to any given stimuli, and we regulate or create a law that's going to overload our already overloaded systems because the law or because the bill may not be specific. I think that to allow the juries to figure it out in this particular case might tie all of us up in court for the rest of our lives.

Taylor: Very possible.

Hayes: And I think that's a great danger here because of that generalization.

Taylor: Representative Merrill has joined us and we are really pleased to have you here this evening. We'll pass this all to you. Thank you very much for coming.

Kirkwood: Representative Francis Merrill.

Merrill: Thank you.

Kirkwood: Now, you're the primary sponsor of this bill, aren't you?

Merrill: Right.

Kirkwood: Okay. There seems to be some questions about the intent of this bill. Is this the broad, encompassing bill that's going to go after things that the bill isn't designed to do or has the Attorney General's office gone over this with you? I assume they have.

Merrill: No, I have not gone in to them to get an opinion.

Kirkwood: Okay, then, what are your feelings? Obviously, Virgil Hayes here has been stating that he feels that this bill is what, much too broad? Representative Merrill, what's your feeling on this? You're sponsoring it, so you obviously have some feelings.

Merrill: Okay, let me tell you where I'm coming from on this bill. I was approached to see if I would be interested in sponsoring this type of legislation and after looking into it I came to the conclusion that it's a subject that needs to be heard, and I'm willing to sponsor it and introduce it up there. Terry Jessop is going to be the spokesman. He is the one that's going to defend it up there. When they ask questions, he's the one that will answer them if they have constitutional questions. The legislative attorneys will be there to answer those and that's the perspective that I am coming from. I think it's a subject that needs to be heard.

Kirkwood: Okay, so you're just a general sponsor rather than specific.

Merrill: That's right.

Kirkwood: Okay, so I guess you need to be here and discuss from your point of view, but coming back to Terry Jessop, you're the primary spokesman.

Merrill: That's right.

Kirkwood: Okay, then Terry, Virgil's comments, let's get some reaction to them.

Jessop: Yes. As we have sat down, whenever one of these bills has been written, the attorneys will always put anything that is germane when it has to do with the Constitution....I cannot speak for Mr. Taggert, but as he has spoken with me in the past, he said, "If this legislation is challenged, it would be challenged on the free speech issue, etc." The reason why he feels that it probably would be found constitutional is that we are not prohibiting the use of subliminals. The major emphasis is that an individual has a right to prior notification and that's the basic image that is being presented on a professional basis. We see no reason why a responsible, ethical person, whether it's for commercial use or any other use, would be opposed to giving prior notification, at least that [consumers] are going to be subjected to subliminals.

Hayes: We are in agreement with the intent of the bill, and as I stated to begin with, we are not here to defend subliminals; however, the definition states something entirely different. If you even look at the dictionary definitions of the words that are used in that definition, being so incredibly broad they are not directed towards any specific purpose. But yet, it could be interpreted through any millions of interpretations and that's where the greatest danger lies in this proposal; not in the intent, but in the proposal itself in the writing of the bill.

Taylor: Now, if I may interject here. Representative Merrill and Terry, I had the opportunity to speak I believe with the co-sponsor, Representative Lloyd Selleniet, and if I understood him correctly, your position on the bill was, it's the intent that is, the object of it: if there were an entanglement, if there were an ambiguity, if there were a problem—and I think I heard you say this earlier, Terry—with a word or with the terminology (if it were too broad, too all-encompassing), you are sensible and you are flexible about it; you would change that or rework it. I'm curious; would that be in the committee or would that be on the floor of the House?

Merrill: Everything is going to be heard in committee tomorrow. All the opposition to it will come in and speak; we will do our little pitch during the committee meeting and I would welcome anybody that is interested in it to come up there and testify whether they're for it or against it. My feeling is it needs to be heard and we would hope that people that are interested in it would come up there. We don't want to pass some law up there that is not going to be good for the people. So, I would say tomorrow is the big day. It may not get out of committee; nobody knows that. We have to wait till tomorrow to see what happens. But we are going to present it and I think if they hear the pros and cons of it, they will make the decision that's right for the people, the state of Utah.

Hayes: Well, according to and going back to what I was saying before, all communication basically contains subliminal elements. Let's say that there proportionately would be absolutely no communication without subliminal elements. I think that you need to write the bill so that it would be appropriately directed towards the specific application such as the 1 percent that are unethical that you had talked about today in the paper. If the 99 percent is being subjected to this bill when in essence it's only 1 percent that is creating the problem, I think that that might be the same situation as using atom bombs to take care of the situation when hand grenades would do.

Jessop: Now, once again, you're still misquoting from the position that was given out of the newspaper. I was talking about advertising agencies, not about subliminal messages per se; basically we feel, I personally feel, that there is a multi-billion-dollar industry out there. Somebody is paying for these subliminals to be produced and it's an extremely expensive type of creation of subliminals. These are being created in television advertisements, motion pictures, etc. Somebody is footing the bill and so I don't believe that by any means that it's only 1 percent of negative subliminals which are encroaching upon our society. If that were the case, perhaps I would not feel so strongly about petitioning very responsible legislators like Representatives Merrill and Selleniet to introduce this legislation. If I could just continue on with this thought. One of the other things that I felt strongly about is, recently there has been a great amount of notoriety having to do with mass-murder slayers, the night stalker in California and many others across the United States, which have been involved in not only mass murders of women but of children, etc. As many people are aware, or perhaps as the populace out there may not be aware, in the background of some music and other programs, there are very strong antisocial messages which maybe say smoke pot, take drugs, commit sexual advances on another person as well as direct commands to kill children, etc. I believe very strongly that an individual that can prove in a court of law that, for example, say the survivors of the family of the child that has been killed, can prove that there has been significant evidence that that murderer was influenced substantially enough, should be able to sue the estate of that particular murderer. That's one of the reasons (and that's not the only reason) why we're not going after, for example, the specific recording industry. That is just one example. The technology is very high tech and it's not limited only to the recording industry and that's why, one of the reasons why I feel uncomfortable in trying to create a law only for the recording industry, only for the television industry, etc., but we had discussed this with the attorneys prior to initiating the legislation.

Hayes: I wonder if you are even aware of the tremendous implications behind what you are actually saying, because, as you are aware, there are many more positive uses than negative ones for subliminal signals. Let's say, to be more specific, a section would require a disclaimer any time that a communication was made of the existence of a subliminally embedded communication, i.e., all communication by anyone who spoke, projected an image, facial expressions, type of clothes, etc., wrote a letter, read a newspaper, sat in church or school. Isn't prayer subliminally embedded communication as well as learning in school? Are these people to be required, if this proposed bill is not defeated now, to provide notice of intent, a written description of possible interpretation on the part of the receiver of the possible responses they might have? Basically, that's the interpretation literally in this bill.

Jessop: No, I think that that's a very radical interpretation which is not reasonably projected at all.

Taylor: Back in the fifties we became aware of subliminal technology primarily through the notoriety that was involved when a New Jersey theater flashed "drink Coca-Cola," "eat popcorn," some such thing on Kim Novak's face during a Kim Novak movie. Now, I know that I've talked to hundreds of people that believe there is legislation in place that protects the consumer against covert manipulation via the modality of subliminal techniques, but it's my understanding that that legislation has always broken down.

Jessop: That's correct, Eldon. Actually, many laws have been introduced all over the United States. As I was working with the former attorney general of the state of Utah, we were not able to find any laws which had actually been enacted anywhere in the United States. However, during the last year several bills are in various forms at least in California, New York, New Jersey, and Pennsylvania. There are some codes saying we would recommend that you don't do this or we would recommend you don't do that, but as far as actually having anyone ever go to jail, pay a fine, or whatever, I am not aware of any actual legislation which has been passed in the United States.

Merrill: The attorneys who drafted the bill think it is constitutional. I personally am concerned about the privacy of my own mind. And I don't want to have that invaded. That's why I am interested in these bills. So I'm interested to see what the discussion is tomorrow and nobody can give the answer. If it ever goes to court on any of these issues, there is a jury probably that will decide the outcome of it. I can't predict that and neither can anybody else.

Kirkwood: I think Representative Merrill is representing a lot of us who are very concerned. I was just complaining to my wife about a week ago about a television commercial; the light comes off of a young body in a way that she looks very ordinary but the light hits her and it's a subliminal message and it's very sexual. And this is what's going on on television and I think, how do you fight that?

Hayes: Well, I think that it might be far more appropriate rather than attempting to legislate morality for an example...

Kirkwood: No, no, no, no. . . .

Hayes: ...that what we might want to attempt to do is educate the individual how to utilize the conscious

40

functioning so that they can reject those ideas at a time when it's appropriate for them because isn't the H.B. 106, 107, and 108 in and of itself an invasion of privacy of those who do choose to indulge in that type of programming?

Kirkwood: All legislation is morality.

Taylor: I don't think it's an invasion of privacy, as a matter of fact. I think what they're asking for is just labeling and I'm all for that.

Jessop: Prior notification is what we're after.

Taylor: If you want to buy a record that is by a heavy-metal group that has "smoke marijuana," "kill a baby" on it, okay. I guess consenting adults, I don't know. Maybe that's even being treated. What you mentioned on television, Jim, that's an issue I think is called superliminal. Through association very often we will see a politician with a flag behind him, you're going to be aware of that flag. Well, that's subliminal in a sense, but it's been defined, as I understand it, as superliminal because the conscious mind has the capability of recognizing the purpose of that association. But when you mention what you see on television, Terry has, as I understand it, an audio-video presentation that will be shown to the legislative committee tomorrow, as well as anyone and everyone that is there. I've seen some of the slides and of course we've talked about some of Professor Key's work *Clam Plate Orgy* and *Subliminal Seduction*, and I've seen some of the material on slides straight out of those books. It's a very real menace to our society. Are we really opposed to that?

Following the radio broadcast, two amendments were offered by Representative Merrill. They were:

House
Committee Amendments
January 29, 1986

Representative Merrill proposes the following amendments to H.B. 106, Subliminal Communication As Invasion of Privacy.

Page 1, Lines 19-22: Delete Section 78-17-1 in its entirety and insert the following in its place:

78-17-1. "Subliminally embedded communication" means any visual image, writing, or sound which is intentionally placed in any printed, audio, or visual medium in order to draw attention to the subject of the medium without the visual image, writing, or sound being consciously perceived, or in order to directly convey or attempt to convey a message which is not consciously perceived. It does not include images or impressions which are conveyed by implication or by visual images or a series of visual images which are consciously perceived.

Utah H.B. 106

Subject: Subliminal Communication as Invasion of Privacy

Suggested amendments:

Add as Section 78-17-6 (page 3 of the Bill):

78-17-6. The provisions of this chapter shall not apply to any entity whose only participation in the conveyance of such messages is as a provider of facilities or services for the transmission of communications to the public.

The Committee heard final statements before issuing a vote. The spokesperson on behalf of the Mind Mint delivered the following summary:

Thank you, Mr. Chairman and Representatives. I'm Annette Hamilton Taylor and the President of JAR, Inc., parent company of the Mind Mint system.

We have two Mind Mint locations in Salt Lake City and are a Utah-based corporation.

The Mind Mint specializes in self-help products and as such offers over three hundred different audio and/or video subliminal products. We are the largest direct retailer of subliminal programs in the country. Everyday I hear testimonies regarding the efficacy of our subliminal products—we know subliminals work.

It has been argued that they do not and even suggested that it takes a dirty mind to find the "alleged subliminal." It has been stated that there is no scientific evidence regarding subliminals. These statements are simply untrue. There is an abundance of literature regarding subliminals. One recent *scientific* study, conducted by Dr. Hal Becker, former professor of Tulane University, exposed subjects to numbers subliminally. Where this was done the subjects scored 80 percent correctly when asked to identify the numbers. (May I add that three-digit numbers were used). Chance alone was less than 20 percent based upon the multiple-choice nature of the selection alternatives. And in groups where subliminals were not used, only about 10 percent identified the three-digit numbers correctly.

Now, as far as the dirty-mind argument is concerned: That is an argument of association. In other words, if you and I find a subliminal that is a taboo, a sex embed, we must have a dirty mind. So what—we pretend not to see what we see? That sounds like conscious repression to me. And as far as subliminals found in some heavy-metal recordings like "Smoke M.J." and "Commit Suicide," even *60 Minutes* has presented exposés documenting this.

In the mid-1950s a New Jersey theater owner claimed to increase coke sales 58 percent via subliminals. The controversy resulted in over forty states introducing some kind of legislation—none of which ever became law. There have always been essentially three arguments that have defeated it. They are:

1. The "dirty-mind argument."

2. The "they don't work argument," and that is interesting with the scientific and clinical data now available, for if they don't work, why oppose them?

3. Finally, the vague and ambiguous argument, that I have saved for last. Yes, the language by definition of subliminal communication is too broad in its extreme sense of interpretation. Twenty-eight years later, there still exists *no* definition to communicate what we all know is trying to be communicated in the intent of Representative Merrill's bills. But someone has to define it.

There are some bills that need to be exposed to rigorous debate and amendment from the entire floor of the House. This is one such bill. There is no technology with more Orwellian possibilities than subliminal communication. We are all entitled to be informed of what subliminal manipulation is present and when present.

There are no virtues to deliberate exploitation by any means, including the intentional misuse of subliminal communication. For that reason we support H.B. 106 and 107.

Thank you.

The Committee narrowly approved the proposed legislation, albeit the House floor did not. Thus, there still exists no legal protection against subliminal invasion!

CHAPTER 4

TESTIMONIES

Thousands of personal testimonies exist concerning subliminal self-improvement tapes. Literally every manufacturer of subliminals sells their product to some extent based upon personal testimonies.

Science is not fond of testimonies per se. A number of variables, including the well-known placebo effect, dilute the "scientific" value of any testimony. Science often scoffs at claims based upon personal experience. To most scientists, where the scientific method and adequate controls are absent, so is the credibility of the experience.

The interesting double bind here is that science now knows there is not such a thing as the observed without the observer and, moreover, the observer is a participant in the event being observed. Nevertheless, science argues for a difference between trained and untrained observers.

Further, science observes phenomena and then applies function, direction, and sometimes other implicate data giving rise to assumed purpose.

A dear friend of mine, Doctor William Guillory, a professor of physical chemistry, has on many occasions flatly asserted that there are no "truths" in science. Science itself is a tautology.

Life is a phenomenon when one considers that at the moment of death no *physical* quality has changed—not weight, not chemistry—yet life is gone. Life itself appears to be metaphysical. Our most basic assumptions are based upon principles that in and of themselves cannot be proven or explained except by observation.

Chapters 5 and 6 treat scientific proof, but it is my opinion that user testimony is not only credible, but of additional value in ascertaining the most meaningful areas to direct any scientific research. People often report a resistance problem, for example, to a particular something or other. Science should then examine this something or other.

To me science is and should be like the FDA. They are there to protect us, very often from our own ignorance, and to improve conditions for all of us. These are consumer-based functions.

Therefore, the user dictates what is or is not meaningful and science attests to the independent or universal validity.

The fact that a placebo alters body chemistry just as pharmacology might, for an individual or a certain percentage of individuals, makes a statement that is meaningful to all, not the least of which is the individual experiencing relief from some physiological dysfunction. When the placebo provides the same relief for the vast majority as pharmacology, it is no longer a placebo. Rather, science should examine further its properties to ascertain the whys and hows inherent in the universal application and the resulting relief brought about by its properties.

To this writer, genius in science is always found where the scientist investigates anomalies. Breakthroughs come from looking more at exceptions than at rules. Thus, I justify the selection of the following testimonies:

I lost weight.
I quit smoking.
My children stopped bed-wetting.
I am always relaxed now.
I sleep soundly.
I feel good.

Testimonial 1
Marilee had over two hundred warts on her hands. Over the years she had many of them burned off. After using a subliminal wart-removal tape for thirty days, the warts were all gone. Six months later the warts had not returned.

Testimonial 2
Mrs. A. H. used a subliminal bust-enlargement tape for thirty days. Her breast size increased from 32A to 34C. One year later the breast size remained 34C.

Testimonial 3
Mike Anglesey chewed his nails down to the quick for fifteen years. A number of stop/prevention programs had been tried by Anglesey. After three weeks of listening to a stop-nail-biting tape, he stopped and had not restarted six months later.

Testimonial 4

Judee Goddard purchased a weight-loss tape to play surreptitiously to her husband. After thirty days, Mr. Goddard had lost twenty-six pounds. Mrs. Goddard did not inform her husband of the subliminal and as of this writing still has not.

Testimonial 5

An unidentified woman reported playing her weight-loss subliminal while preparing dinner. After several exposures, she observed that her twenty-month-old baby had stopped eating his dinner. She discontinued use of the tape while her child was present.

Where children are concerned, when a word becomes meaningful as a word is an area of relevant inquiry. Peter Eimas of Brown University has amassed considerable evidence suggesting that a child one month of age can distinguish some differences in words. In light of this, the question of subliminal exposure to very young children takes on a different dimension.

Testimonial 6

To placate his wife, Dempsey Whitaker, a heavy smoker for thirty-eight years, agreed to listen to a subliminal stop-smoking tape. Whitaker stated that he was not ready to stop smoking, but he would listen to the tape. After seven days, Whitaker no longer wanted a cigarette, and one year later Whitaker remains a nonsmoker.

Testimonial 7

Mrs. X was involved in an auto accident. Physical therapy was required for rehabilitation. The therapy, basically stretching exercises, was impossible for Mrs. X until her daughter purchased a joy of exercise subliminal, after which the therapy was accomplished without psychological or physiological side effects.

Testimonial 8

Vern Waters's mother, a social worker, purchased a stop-loss-of-hair tape for Vern. Vern had already lost most of his hair in what appeared to be a classical male pattern baldness experience. After listening for less than one month, Vern began to grow new hair. After approximately two months, Vern once again had a full head of hair.

Testimonial 9
Arnold Stringham suffered from migraine headaches for years. After using a subliminal migraine-relief tape for less than thirty days, the headaches ceased.

So convinced is Stringham of the efficacy of these tapes that he now uses subliminals in a real estate school he instructs, and claims a statistically significant increase in the number of students passing the state examination as a result. Stringham's first day of instruction with a new class is partially spent explaining subliminals, relating his experiences, recommending the tapes, and then commencing to play various learning programs.

This author has heard testimonies from hundreds of subliminal users purporting to improve memory, test-taking skills, learning abilities, and concentration; to remove warts, end migraines, enlarge breasts, promote healing; to end insomnia, provide relief from allergies, and so on. Many times I have been asked, "How does a tape do this?" The tapes do not *do* anything other than provide the mind with stimuli that the mind acts upon. The mind is the doer!

CHAPTER 5

THE CLINICAL DATA

I n Chapter 2 eight areas of human activity were identified as having been demonstrably affected by subliminal communication. Once again, these areas are:

1. Conscious perception
2. Dreams
3. Drives
4. Emotions
5. Memory
6. Perceptual defenses
7. Value norm anchor points
8. Verbal behavior

In *Subliminal Seduction*, Professor Key illustrates each of these areas as they are affected and even exploited via subliminal massaging techniques. This author highly recommends Key's work; however, the nature of my volume is not so much to look at media exploitation as to distinguish the hype from the credible, hence only a cursory review of Key's material is appropriate here.

Conscious perception presupposes that the way one sees the world is within a system of "sets." Most behavioral scientists credit the enculturation process with this predisposition. The sets are often referred to by political scientists as ethnocentric. Means for coping and evaluating good and bad, right and wrong within a society are constructed through the use of sets.

For example, facial expressions and body language in general are often paired with the use of language to give rise to different meanings. According to Key, interpretation of facial expressions has been demonstrated to be influenceable by subliminal stimuli. In other words, a basically expressionless face can be seen as an angry expression if the viewer is exposed simultaneously to the word *anger* at a subliminal level.

Dreams constitute one of our clearest empirical accesses to unconscious processes. As was discussed earlier when reviewing some of Poetzle's work, dreams often process subliminally perceived stimuli. Key cites several instances of individuals dreaming "out" subliminally perceived stimuli from researchers' work with particular taboo embeds found in commercial advertising. Key also suggests that subliminal perception is a close kin to posthypnotic suggestion. Since posthypnotic suggestions can and often are erased from conscious awareness by another suggestion for partial amnesia, Key suggests that the functional aspect of both are more alike than not.

As a hypnotist, I am aware of a number of applications where subliminal communication is employed simultaneously with trance therapy to effect beneficial changes in a client. Very often for light hypnotic subjects a dichotic approach is preferred. For example, a hypnotherapist may use a verbal dialogue suggesting to the client that it's okay to feel good about themselves while simultaneously playing a subliminal audio track under gentle ocean sounds that is flatly stating, "I do feel good about myself."

Dreams very often are passages to otherwise hidden unresolved conflict. It is not at all uncommon for a therapist to have a dream reported that brings this conflict to the surface after a session utilizing a dichotic or amnesive approach as an uncovering technique; but that can also be said for any other normally acceptable therapeutic intervention or uncovering modality.

Emotions are among the most responsive of all human behavioral characteristics to be affected by subliminal communication. The ability of subliminal input to excite, arouse, anger, or desensitize external stimuli is well established in the literature and will be discussed in more detail later in this chapter when we look at specific clinical data.

Memory also has been increased by the aid of subliminal perception. The Lozanov material was discussed earlier. The "superlearning" formats as they have become known (due largely to the work of Lynn Schroeder and Sheila Ostrander), whether called suggestology, suggestopedia, sophrology, or accelerated learning, usually incorporate both some form of altered (alpha) consciousness and subliminal technology.

It should also be noted that memory is a complex process. Ordinarily, when referring to memory the discussion is about conscious memory, but there exists also unconscious memory.

Since our defense mechanisms function the way they do, many memories become undesirable and are stored away in the unconscious. It can be further said that many one-time useful memories have also slipped out of conscious memory into the subconscious/unconscious. There is also unconscious processing going on that the conscious never was aware of. These are unconscious memories.

The exploiters of subliminal technology usually will appeal more to the unconscious level of memory in their manipulative merchandising. If the amount of money spent on this kind of merchandising is any reflection of the success ratio for this type of marketing strategy, this form of subliminal communication is very effective.

There is also associative memory. That is, memory of something consciously perceived because of stimuli simultaneously unconsciously perceived and yet connectively associated. One good, although in this author's opinion irresponsible, example of this can be illustrated by the work of educational psychologist Dr. Bruce R. Ledford. Ledford theorized that if advertisers could increase product identification, then in a similar manner, learning could be enhanced.

Ledford proceeded to expose students at East Texas State University to erotic and violent pictures projected subliminally on a screen behind him. The slides were shown at one candle-power above the light in the classroom and were therefore consciously imperceptible.

Ledford's lectures, which had nothing to do with the slides being projected, were apparently more interesting to the students than in the past, as reflected by test scores. Test results indicated a significant increase in memory relevant to the material presented by Ledford, as compared to students of a control group who viewed only a blank screen behind Ledford's lectures.

Perceptual defenses protect us from shocking or deeply traumatic material. Our perceptual defenses can actually assist a subliminal manipulation by shutting out data one might otherwise perceive. Tantamount to this is Key's example of the Howard Johnson menu in his *Clam Plate Orgy*. An orgy scene is not what one expects to find in an illustration of a plate of clams on a menu in a prominent and respected restaurant. Simply speaking, we refuse to see what is there to be seen.

Value norm anchor points are positions selected by an individual as a referent point between opposites. It is from these points that one evaluates himself and the world around him. It is a personally/culturally accepted position between good and bad, right and wrong, success and failure, approval and rejection, and so forth. Numerous studies report that subliminally perceived data can move these anchor points around.

As a criminologist, for years I regularly interacted with what society refers to as thieves, criminals, etc. One thing I observed quickly: no one believes himself to be bad. Now that may be an overgeneralization, but essentially everyone rationalizes away deviant behavior through one or more of the defense mechanisms.

Truth requires facing responsibility at some level of reality. Accepting self-responsibility is more often than not counter to the motives of our defense mechanisms.

Have you ever asked yourself why a person confesses a crime? I have conducted hundreds of lie detection tests and have taken hundreds of confessions. Not once did the examinee come into my office with a confession on his or her lips. Denial, denial, denial is the point at which all interrogations begin.

A good interrogator learns to read every aspect of communication, from word count to body language. They also understand and use the defense mechanisms. For example, an interrogator may suggest to a person suspected of stealing from an employer that the employer is harsh and unfair, thereby affording the suspect empathy and an opportunity to rationalize his or her behavior by placing blame on the employer. In other words, the employer deserved it! Had he been fair, he would have paid the suspect more and not stolen time and taken advantage of the employee to the extent that it became okay to "get even" with the employer.

In a discussion one day with an associate of mine, he informed me of a subliminal study that had been conducted in conjunction with the use of lie detection. This piqued my interest. Could a subliminal be used to soften a value norm anchor point and produce a new reference on the truthful end of the truth/lie compendium? Despite my efforts to locate the study, I was never successful. Nevertheless, I decided to try an experiment on my own. The subliminal I selected was commercially available from a company called Mind Communications. The subliminal audio tape contained harp and flute music with subaudible words from the 23rd Psalm.

I observed immediate differences in length of interrogation time, confession ratios to deception indicated charts, and pretest admissions. The 23rd Psalm had made my work much easier. Why would the 23rd Psalm move a moral valuing anchor point in our culture? To me the answer is obvious and the real question is: Would it do the same in a non-Christian culture? One other noticeable difference was evident with the use of the 23rd Psalm. Situational stress and general anxiety levels of all subjects was reduced.

Now, this is experiential data—not scientific proof. However, two other examiners have reported similar findings to me as a result of using this same subliminal audio cassette.

Verbal behavior is a complex construct. To the extent of interest within the scope of subliminal use, there are at least three aspects to be considered:

1. Multiple meaning permutations
2. Explicit/implicit set
3. Contextual reference

Multiple meaning permutations refer to words which contain other words with drastically different meanings. Consider the "con" in confidence. This category also refers to implications or associations, such as the vegetable *pea* and verb *pee*. Key, in *Subliminal Seduction*, states that certain taboo four-letter words are also implied in seemingly innocuous verbage. Key selected such words as whose (whore) and cult (cunt) to demonstrate strong emotional responses at a subliminal level. Key claims that words of this nature are deliberately used in ad copy to build emotional content. Key also refers to a broad scope of experiments that demonstrate that these emotion-laden words evoke physiological responses that can be measured on an electro-encephalograph.

Explicit/implicit and contextual reference in verbal response and behavior are discussed in Chapter 7 which discusses subliminal modalities.

A number of other areas of human activity that subliminal communication can and does affect are suggested by clinical data.

The Soviets are reported to have been working on subliminal condition/response for years. Subliminals can influence skin temperature, galvanic response, heartbeat—in fact, nearly if not all of one's physiological processes.

In 1983, I spoke with Owen Stitz of Mid-West Research, and he reported to me that they had created a subliminal for use by law enforcement personnel in terrorist abductions, that it had been tested, and that it worked. The subliminal was designed to bring about dysfunctions of the bladder, liver, and kidneys.

Stitz explained that where terrorist abductions were concerned, statistics indicated that a number of hours were spent on the phone in negotiation with the terrorists. The idea was to create a subliminal and cover the audio-track with pink sound—in this instance, the sound of air conditioning. Stitz claimed that the tape was tested at an unidentified police academy under medical supervision, but employed covertly. After three days, the subliminal was removed. The result of the test was that nearly the entire class of cadets had become dehydrated.

Subliminals have been demonstrated to affect the perception threshold. Ostrander and Schroeder relate in their *Subliminal Report* that when words with unsavory connotations were subliminally presented to one eye, it increased the perception threshold of the other eye.

Subliminals can influence addictive behavior. Psychologist Thomas Budzynski studied subliminal input and its effect on alcoholics. Groups treated with subliminals and therapy responded significantly better than the group receiving therapy only. Budzynski has applied for a federal grant to study further the role of specific suggestions in subliminal scripts.

Behavior therapy is one of the major avenues for subliminal use. Such behavioral modification therapy has been applied in areas as diverse as jet lag and agoraphobia. One interesting clinical approach, as an example, was that taken by Dr. Dominic Marino. Treating a fifty-eight-year-old patient who feared thunderstorms, Marino used subliminal messages as part of a multifaceted means to effect alleviation of behavior associated with thunderstorms. Marino reported that the thunderstorm phobia was completely eliminated.

Subliminals can relax one or prime one for action. Subliminal research appears to be a field of embryonic stature; that is, subliminal communication is potentially the most powerful form of communication known to man. It also appears that the scope of use for subliminals is limited only by the power of the human mind.

CHAPTER 6

SUBLIMINAL TECHNOLOGY

There exist a number of ways to communicate subliminally. Perhaps before discussing various technical methods it would be wise to differentiate the use of the word *subliminal* a little more than has been done. If you recall the legislative debate, *subliminal* technically means any form of communication not consciously perceived. For purposes here, the following stratification of word usage and meaning shall apply:

Supraliminal, meaning perceivable, albeit generally not to the conscious mind. Associations, such as a politician and a baby and/or contextual inferences are examples.

Subception, referring to something ordinarily not perceivable by the conscious mind due to the operation of one or more defense mechanisms. An example would be a taboo embed, such as that used by *Playboy's* subscription ad and the wreath of genitalia already discussed.

Subliminal is defined as that which *cannot* be assessed by the conscious mind due to some technical application that masks the accessibility, except perhaps by technical unmasking capabilities being first applied.

Now, with these definitions in place, supraliminal communication covers ordinary communication that may have unconscious communication inherent to it and subception refers to manipulation of the kind sometimes used by advertisers in print media. Both of these forms of communication are accessible to the trained observer without the technical assistance of special equipment or instrumentation. It would appear to this author that legislating against them would seriously endanger our freedom of speech by establishing further precedents impeding free speech. In other words, we already have obscenity and pornography statutes, and should an advertisement be deemed obscene or pornographic, the jurisprudence process is equipped to deal with it. (This might be an interesting avenue in which to pursue some subliminal manipulators.)

Subliminal, then, refers to communication created by technical assistance (e.g., equipment, instruments, technology in general) that simply cannot be perceived directly by the conscious mind irrespective of the training or sophistication about such matters by the observer. For example, if a sound engineer back-masks a spoken message in a heavy-metal recording, creating a subliminal stimuli to the listener, he does not possess the conscious ability to perceive the subliminal in the finished product any more than any other listener, without technical assistance from special instrumentation.

It appears easier to create legislation that is not a constitutional infringement and that would protect the public from this kind of exploitation when these definitions of subliminal communication are understood.

Subliminal stimuli can be perceived at many sensory levels. Low-voltage electrical shock has been used to bring about responses when the voltage was too low for the recipient to have awareness of the shock conditioning. The neurophone developed by Dr. Patrick Flanagan has been demonstrated to electronically induce suggestions by skin contact. Dick Sutphen claims that when this instrument was shown to the National Security Agency, they promptly confiscated it.

Literally every sense can be appealed to subliminally, but the two most often used are those that reach either the audio or video senses. Generally, video subliminal stimuli is generated in one of three ways:

1. Slide insertion
2. Candlepower ratio levels
3. Tachistoscope projection

Slide insertion is essentially what was reportedly used in the theater houses in New Jersey. A slide may be inserted as often as one per fourteen frames and usually go consciously unnoticed. A simple visual method for understanding this technique can be produced with a fast-turn card deck, the kind children used to make. By inserting any message once every fourteen to twenty-eight frames and then by thumbing the deck rapidly, one can replicate the type of subliminal exposure involved in the slide insertion process.

Candlepower ratio levels are of the type discussed earlier with Dr. Ledford's erotica and violence. Simply lowering the wattage output and/or connecting a rheostat to a person's home projector to produce light slightly above that of the room will replicate this process. In fact, it might make for an interesting home experiment to do this with a slide projector and then project a message such as "I like to study" behind the television set while the teenagers are glued to MTV.

Tachistoscope projection is accomplished by a device that flashes messages every five seconds at a speed of 1/3000th of a second. An ordinary projector with a high-speed shutter can be modified to produce this effect. Ordinarily speaking, the candle-power method is more effective than the tachistoscope, simply because the message is continuous. The tachistoscope itself was patented in 1967 (Patent No. 3,060,795) by Precon Process and Equipment Corporation of New Orleans.

According to Key in *Subliminal Seduction*, the device was originally used to flash subliminal messages on television and on theater screens. Key states that this was the method used by at least one theater during a six-week period to expose 45,699 patrons to the subliminals "Drink Coca-Cola" and "Hungry? Eat Popcorn."

Key states that a survey research check conducted during July 1971 located thirteen commercial firms that (for the right price) could and would offer subliminal services to advertisers. What is more frightening, the targeted survey was of only three markets: New York, Chicago, and Toronto.

There are a number of modalities involved in audio-subliminal projection as well. Perhaps the best known is the "black box," a device that Professor Becker patented in 1969. Essentially, the most popular methods are:

1. Becker's black box
2. Psychoacoustical concealment
3. Back-masking or metacontrast
4. White-sound masking

There are a number of methods derived from each of the four and some overlapping, as further discussion will reveal. In addition, there is great debate over the speed of messages as in time-compressed modalities and the frequency bands used to modulate the subliminal, especially where inexpensive players are used to review the content.

The commercial marketplace is full of "snake oil" salespeople. Audio subliminals have created a new industry in America, selling instant fixes for everything from poverty to obesity. Many of these companies are peddling absolute panaceas in their claims, implicitly if not explicitly. Some have adopted the old "more is better" mentality and there appears to be open competition over who can get the most affirmations on a single tape.

In this author's opinion, subliminal self-help is here to stay. Not only that, but in the very near future it will represent a major preferred method for effecting beneficial change. However, just as subliminals are *not* the invisible and therefore nonexistent yet pretended to be perceived emperor's clothes, they are also *not* a panacea. There are definite limitations and even contraindications to their use. Be this as it may, it is the informed consumer that eventually will decide what companies will remain in business when the initial awe of new technology is replaced by consumer awareness.

Becker's "black box" processes spoken words into music by simply averaging the volume levels of the music and producing the spoken word as a subliminal slightly beneath the music volume. Ordinarily, tracings of this process show the following:

However, since the process and its various derivations use averages, it is not at all uncommon to produce the following tracing:

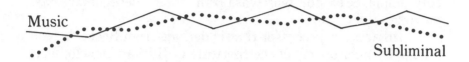

Music

Subliminal

It can be seen that the subliminal content may thus become audible or semiaudible during part of the programming.

Becker's process was tested in a supermarket in New Orleans during 1979. the "black box" mixed "Thou shalt not steal" and "Honesty is the best policy" into the Muzak system broadcasted in the store. Reported lowering of cash shortages, inventory damage, and pilferage were astounding.

Becker's resourcefulness as both researcher and entrepreneur led to the creation of weight-loss programs that worked. Not only did the participants lose weight, but their losses were not regained. In 11 percent of the instances, the maintained weight loss was 25 percent, for 50 percent more the maintained loss was 50 percent, and for the remaining 24 percent the maintained loss was between 75 to 100 percent over a two-year period.

It was Becker's process that was used at McDonagh Medical Center and for the most part was used to establish audio-subliminal credibility.

The Becker "black" box is used today by commercial companies to produce audio subliminals available to consumers. One such company is Mind Communication. The format is one of a selection of music or ocean sounds, with Dr. Paul Tuthill introducing the title and reviewing the subliminal content. Mind Communication produces the 23rd Psalm subliminal tape referred to earlier.

One drawback to modern-day use of the Becker "box" is that recordings are monaural.

A very close cousin to Becker's process is one developed by Dr. Louis Romberg. Romberg, a native of East Germany, began researching subliminal communication in the early 1960s. Romberg's device was installed in a Canadian tire store in Toronto. The store offered a line of general hardware. Reportedly, employee productivity was up and thefts were considerably down.

Still another processor that is derived from Becker's technology is the property of the Institute of Human Development and is used to produce a commercial line of tapes.

According to *Subliminal Report* by Schroeder and Ostrander, some fifty retail stores in the United States have introduced subliminals to their background music. It is assumed that the message content deals with antitheft, such as "I am honest."

Psychoacoustical concealment can be accomplished in a number of ways, one of which is to harmonize voice frequency with primary sound output. Sometimes the voice is made to sound like an instrument and sometimes like "pink" or "gray" sound, which is simply background sound such as the "swooshing" of a gentle wind.

One such company reformatting voice frequencies to conceal them in the music is Valley of the Sun. The creator of Valley of the Sun, Dick Sutphen, asserts that when efforts to acquire rights to Becker's "black box" were broken off, he engaged sound engineers in California to develop the process. Sutphen further states that the ease with which they came up with the process was frightening, in view of the fact that the subliminal content cannot then be rediscovered even with the use of sophisticated equipment, including the parametric equalizer.

In effect, white sound mixing and acoustical concealment are nearly the same. The difference is, white sound contains all audible sound frequencies, but pink and gray sound and most specific sounds do not. Therefore, the voice track used to produce the subliminal either must be matched with the frequencies of the pink and gray sound, specific frequencies used by musical instruments, or lowered slightly below the white sound background (usually the sound of ocean surf).

Back-masking usually is accomplished in frequency mixing; however, in this instance the audio track of spoken messages is reversed or played backwards.

Ultrahigh and extra low frequencies can also be incorporated in any of these formats. The silent dog whistle is a simple example of a frequency not consciously perceived by the human ear and yet verifiably perceived by the human's unconscious or subconscious processes.

There are many other twists to the modalities outlined here and some of the actual techniques are either considered trade secrets or patented processes.

Sound engineer Glen Pace has had personal experience with both high- and low-frequency mixing and back-masking. In a conversation with Glen in August 1986, he candidly discussed with this author his earliest subliminal experience. Glen was a recording engineering and record producer for about eighteen years. At one time he was probably one of the top five recording engineers in Los Angeles. Glen now makes his home in Texas. He has also been involved in the studio building business and therefore has contributed to several of the top studios around the country.

Glen states that he first got involved with subliminals back in the late sixties and early seventies when approached by some of the heavy-metal groups.

In *Subliminal Seduction* Key claims that one of the objectives of heavy-metal recordings is popularity with the young people by appealing to their desire to torment adults, their parents in particular. Key further asserts that a manipulation of loud/soft value anchoring points was accomplished by injecting subaudible sounds, tones, and harmonics at levels that encouraged turning up the volume. Certain sounds, especially those recorded in the bass ranges, become audible by increasing the volume of the recording.

Pace was told that the idea for subliminal back-masking was an old Eastern idea. Pace was aware that the mind reverses what it perceives. The idea was to play backwards messages that the mind would reverse. That idea is worth interrupting the continuity of our story for a moment.

The nature of our language is such that a single word often contains opposites. Think of the "sin" in sincere or remember the "con" in confidence. Then there are words such as Marshall McLackan cites in the introduction to *Subliminal Seduction*, words like *eros* and *live*. When these words are reversed, the meaning is drastically changed. Eros becomes sore and live

69

becomes evil. It therefore becomes a valid, albeit irritating, question of whether or not heavy-metal groups using satanic subliminals are corrupting or evangelizing their audiences.

Glen stated to me that at that time he couldn't have cared less about what they were doing—all he cared about was that they paid his bill. That is not at all where Glen Pace stands today. A deeply religious man, Glen is committed to the use of subliminal technology for the benefit of mankind. Glen has a studio in Texas where he creates subliminals. He and Dr. Tom Budzynski plan a scientific study regarding back-masking and he has been asked to become involved with the Alabama Prison system to conduct some subliminal research there.

Glen believes he was one of the first few engineers to be involved in the "backwards" thing. Glen said that he heard the groups discuss research from the Far East but never actually saw any of it.

Originally, the back-masking was recorded on a monaural or two tracks, turned around, and blended in.

Glen told this author that in "a few years of watching it, knowing about it, it definitely had some merit to it . . . ." Some of the messages were picked up by the kids and "you could see it in their behavior and they would have had no other way of depicting what we put on there." Glen says that the messages included all kinds of things, "everything from 'drugs are great' to satanic types of things." That is where Glen drew the line and refused to be involved. He knows of two or three other engineers that did get involved in recording satanic messages for three of todays most popular rock groups.

Glen's present subliminal process is one of multilayer, multifrequency, using some noteworthy but confidential additional means to enhance the subliminal communication.

Means to create audio subliminal recordings range from the sophisticated use of digital recording equipment to the "home-made" version explained in Chapter 9, with do-it-yourself instructions.

CHAPTER 7

SCIENTIFIC FINDINGS

An argument for subliminal use could begin centuries ago, but that is not the scope of this work. Therefore, the data presented in this chapter are drawn from contemporary findings.

Two of the most notable researchers of subliminal technology and perception are Dr. Norman Dixon, author of *Preconscious Processing*, a veritable text on the subject for professionals, and Dr. Lloyd Silverman of New York University.

Where subliminal stimuli is concerned, Dixon has probably participated in more explorations of a diverse nature than anyone else. His research in the area has resulted in the formulation of certain generalizations. Dixon asserts that being conscious is not the same as information processing. There are at least two systems, one of which the conscious is unaware of. Not only that, but the preconscious processor, the unconscious, performs tasks that formerly were thought to be the province of the conscious. Two examples: information such as the meaning of new words can be processed and integrated with relevant data in the memory and responses can be elicited without stimuli ever circuiting conscious awareness.

Dixon's work is representative of a wide compendium of subliminal application and implications ranging from the traditional stimuli perception to the more classically unorthodox parapsychological.

Dr. Lloyd Silverman has researched subliminals for over twenty years and is heralded by some as the world's foremost academic researcher of subliminal communication.

Silverman's work with symbiotic fantasies has been the breeding ground for a host of new studies and articles. Sometimes referred to as the "Oneness Fantasy," suggestions such as "Mommy and I are one" and "It's okay to do better than daddy" have been demonstrated to possess near-panaceac potential. Everything from learning ability to dart-throwing skills have been improved as a result of exposure to these subliminal messages.

That may seem difficult to believe, but a commonly held idea in psychology is that a merging fantasy (symbiotic fantasy), generally with archetypes, will improve adaptive behavior.

Dr. Silverman first approached subliminal research as a path to understanding the unconscious. Silverman assumed the hypothesis that conflict originating in the unconscious as the result of conflicting wishes gave rise to adaptive behavior. (All behavior is adaptive even if by convention it appears to be maladaptive.) The more serious and unresolved the conflict, the more deviant the behavior.

Silverman proceeded to test his postulate by flashing "psychoactivating subliminals" as he termed them. The theory worked. Schizophrenic symptoms were exacerbated by approximately 70 percent.

The "mommy" message first appeared in journals as the result of its use in a weight-loss class. Dr. Silverman and an associate, Dr. Rose Bryant-Tuckett, applied the "mommy" subliminal to a group of emotionally handicapped youngsters in an informed consent situation at a New York school. No one in the experiment group knew what the message was. The measurement device for achieved results was the California Achievement Reading Test. Silverman and Tuckett designed a control group into their experiment and used the tachistoscope to present the subliminal "mommy and I are one."

Significantly higher scores were achieved by the children who viewed the subliminal than by the control group. In addition, a number of "spillover" gains were associated with the test group. These gains ranged from behavioral improvement to improved class grades in arithmetic.

Not unlike the spillover gains of Silverman and Tuckett's findings, Dr. Kenneth Parker of Queen's College, in an experiment designed to improve academic performance of law students, found that the magic "mommy" message improved academic performance in general. Also using a control group which received neutral messages, Parker demonstrated significant gains on behalf of the test group. Not only this, but after one month those who had received the subliminal message had higher retention of the learning-enhanced material.

A number of attempts by researchers to duplicate the efficacy of the "mommy" subliminal have been made using deviations of the symbiotic fantasy. Such messages as "Daddy and I are one" and "the professor and I are one" proved less effective than the magical "mommy" fantasy.

Dr. Sima Ariam tested the "mommy" subliminal on students in Tel Aviv and discovered that its effect may be cross-cultural. Ariam, a Silverman student, produced findings similar to those produced by his former mentor. The archetypical mommy apparently is not bound just to western culture.

Silverman suggests that, paradoxically, the oneness fantasy with mommy is an archetypal experience with the "good mother of infancy" that produces self-sufficiency. One of the key words to the "mommy" message, however, has been shown to be *one*. The essential aspect of "mommy" power appears to come from the oneness metaphor.

In a recent, yet unpublished finding by Dr. Thomas Budzynski and his wife, doctoral candidate at the University of Paris, Lawrence Doche-Budzynski, "mommy" power was incorporated with "daddy" messages to bring about statistically significant findings. Their experiment was conducted with Type A males. An assumption based on Freidman and others' work that Type A males possess low self-esteem was part of their working hypothesis. Using four statistical measurement scales (the Minnesota Multiphasic Personality Inventory [MMPI], the Jenkin's Attitude Survey, the Tennessee Self-Concept, and the Cooper Self-Esteem), pretesting and post-testing revealed significant increases in subject self-esteem.

Unlike the earlier work of others, the Budzynskis used audio subliminals. The messages "Mommy and I are one," variations of Silverman's "Okay to do better than Dad," and "I am good" were spoken slowly and meaningfully and then masked beneath the gentle sounds of ocean waves. No fancy multitracking, time-compressing, or voice-frequency switching was involved. The experimenters had participants use the audio tape once a day for four weeks. Listening to the program involved approximately twenty minutes each day. The experiment was designed as a double-blind study. After four weeks, testing clearly indicated beneficial gains on behalf of the participants receiving the subliminal. In addition, ninety days later a residual gain remained measurable.

In South Africa, Dr. T. F. Pettigrew presented subjects with subliminals based on brain lateralization experiments. Simultaneously, each eye of the subjects viewed different pictures. While one eye received the slide of a white face, the other was presented with a black face. This dichotic experiment had some interesting results. South Africans were able to assemble the two faces and perceive a face. Native Africans were unable to bring about fusion of the images and to see a face.

Dr. Budzynski's work in the area of audio dichotic subliminals appeals to this hemispheric difference insofar as dominant and minor functions are concerned and perhaps works as well as it does in part due to "blocking" aspects of perception (see Chapters 5 and 6).

One observed claim about the "mommy" subliminal is that it loses its power if conscious awareness becomes attached to its use. It is argued that this is due to the ability of the conscious mind to accept or reject input, a sort of mitigation by conscious awareness effect. Most of the evidence that suggests this derives from research with visually presented subliminal stimuli—pictures and words.

This author has been involved in an audio subliminally presented program with different findings. Working with Charles McCusker and Lee Liston at the Utah State Prison, I developed a subliminal script that incorporated the "mommy" subliminal. Participants reviewed the script before using the cassette program initially.

Liston had approached me regarding the use of subliminal technology for rehabilitation purposes. Liston, an official with the Corrections Department, obtained permission to conduct the research, subject to certain conditions and limitations. McCusker's background in statistical psychology and computerized psychometrics was deemed essential to the project and thus he was drafted.

A double-blind experiment was devised using a waiting control group, a placebo group, and a test group. Two psychological measurement instruments were incorporated for preevaluations and postevaluations.

Anonymity of the volunteer inmates was one of the conditions where the Minnesota Multiphasic Personality Inventory (MMPI) was concerned. Consequently, the MMPI was administered with reference to designated groups only. The Fowler Lense of the MMPI was used to arrive at what the actual subliminal message would be. In that way, the measurement device was not only useful to appraise before and after, but essential to the message selection process.

Approval was granted to use the Thurstone Temperament Scale on an individual basis for preevaluation and postevaluation.

Pretesting resulted in the interpretation that three areas generally reflected by the inmates would constitute the direction of the subliminal script. Those three areas were:

1. Low reflectivity scores
2. Low sociability scores
3. High self-alienation scores

One of our discoveries led us to believe that at least one propensity functioning with this particular volunteer population of inmates (forty in all) was inherent to the way they acted upon "poor self-esteem." It was as if they had decided that their low self-worth was indicative of society's low self-worth. If they weren't worth shit, no one else was either!

Consequently, the subliminal messages were designed to raise their self-appraisals as well as those of society. With a minister's perspective and after some initial objections or reservations by Liston and McCusker regarding at least one of the messages, agreement was achieved. The following affirmations thus became the subliminal content of our programs:

I am calm.
I am relaxed.
I am in control.
I create my future.
I am self-responsible.
I am patient.

I am honest.
I am peaceful.
I am tranquil.
I forgive myself.
I forgive others.
I am positive.
I am responsible.
I am happy.
I am confident.
I am capable.
I can do anything.
I am one with the Divine.
Mommy and I are one.
Honesty is oneness.
I live in oneness.
I like myself.
I like others.
I respect myself.
I respect others.
I love all.
All is oneness.
I am at peace in oneness.

Two identical tapes were created, except that one did *not* contain subliminal content. The affirmations were spoken slowly and deliberately, with meaningful voice inflections. The recordings used two primary carriers: ocean sounds and piano music performed in a pantanic scale. (The music was made available by the Institute of Human Development.)

The project was flawed both by unseen and unexpected circumstances as well as by some of the conditions and limitations imposed by the State Correction system. (A detailed analysis is available from Liston and an abstract of findings written by McCusker appears in the appendix to this work.) Nevertheless, statistically meaningful data were assembled. Due to the success of the project, additional studies are presently under way.

Some of the findings suggest the following conclusions:

1.   The test group did receive significant measurable gain in the specific three areas messages were tailored to address.

2.   There was a degeneration of certain variables relevant to social adjustment, authoritarian problems, and self-esteem in the majority of observations taken from both the placebo and control groups, ostensibly indicating either frustration or reflecting the role of the incarceration environment. Either way, this tends to make positive swings even more statistically significant.

3.   There was a two-to-one ratio of dropout participants from the placebo group as compared with the test group. (Remember, this was conducted strictly on a volunteer basis, right down to the daily checking out of tape and player. No incentives and no coercion techniques were applied.)

4.   The perceived environmental erosion arising from the control and placebo groups would suggest application and/or usage within thirty days of release for highest efficacy.

The nature of this program is designed to interrupt and diminish recidivism rates. Since those statistics are primarily organized in two-year groupings, follow-up on this measurement will not be available for some time yet.

From the Thurstone Temperament Scale some graphic comparisons are worth illustrating (see Figures 1, 2, 3, and 4). (A table of these measurements is provided in Appendix A). Overall analysis for the Thurstone Temperament Scale revealed the following comparisons between the experimental group and the control group (the placebo group comparison was deemed invalid due to insufficient posttest observations) (see Figure 5).

The MMPI indicated general drops in affective variables taken from the basic scales.

As encouraging as this may seem, one aspect revealed by statistical analysis of the MMPI that is alarming, even though the sample size is too small and not enough other data relevant to individual comparisons and/or "experiences" in the incarcerated environment during the twenty-day subliminal project are available, is that of schizophrenic tangential thinking. The control group scored down and the experimental group scored up nearly one full unit of standard deviation where schizophrenic tangential thinking was concerned. The experimental group's increase may suggest a related side effect to the symbiotic fantasy or to some other flaw in the message design. It may also be due to some trauma experienced by one of the participants during this pilot study.

Silverman is quoted by the *Newsletter Perspective* as believing that at least one good ideal in mental health is the ability to vacillate comfortably between union or the oneness fantasy and individuation. Perhaps this movement in urges manifests itself in some via schizophrenic thought processes. That seems highly unlikely to this author; nevertheless, careful observation of this issue appears warranted.

In short, as a result of a plethora of investigations, subliminal communication has earned credibility with the informed. In fact, recent research has the implication of presenting preferred personality types for earliest perception integration. Some researchers suggest a similarity between personality types already associated as "high psi hitters" with subliminal perception.

In one such article appearing in *The Journal of the American Society for Physical Research,* investigator Gertrude R. Schmeidler compared ESP as a normal psychological ability with subliminal perception skills. Her correlation statistics indicate a favorable comparison in that scores on the one can predict scores on the other.

This positive correlation between ESP skills and subliminal perception is one demonstration of what may and will eventually lead to clustering personality types before researching subliminal impact since many of these personality groupings have already been suggested by parapsychologists.

In recapitulation, the question is not whether subliminal communication is "real"; rather, the question appears to be one of how best to employ it to bring about beneficial results.

CHAPTER 8

UNANSWERED QUESTIONS

Despite the rather large body of research in the subliminal field, there remain many more questions than answers, not just for researchers but for consumers.

The ethical consideration is inherently entwined with the issues of legislation and freedom of speech. There is also a question of competency versus freedom in the marketplace where commercial products such as self-improvement audio and video subliminals are concerned. In addition, there is the old question regarding practicing psychology (or medicine) without a license.

One of the oldest (and the largest) retail subliminal manufacturers, Potentials Unlimited, once had their entire inventory seized by U.S. marshals over alleged medical claims. Potentials Unlimited prevailed, but to some extent the issue remains unsolved.

Professor Key believes subliminals are potentially dangerous because they reach directly our deepest reservoirs of behavioral and belief systems.

Add to this subliminal concern the fact that some companies produce video subliminals that are dramas, as opposed to video subliminals that typically feature beautiful nature scenes, and another dimension of concern enters the picture. One such video that I have seen (a very good one in my opinion) is a psychodrama portraying an actress in a weight-loss motivation scenario. This video is manufactured and distributed by Valley of the Sun, but even its superior content from the cognitively observable drama could be argued to have its "practicing psychology" implications.

In a very real sense, all entertainment appeals and persuades at some level to each and every one of our psyches. From entertainment our archvillains and heroes are spawned, our tolerances as a society are expanded, and so forth.

Dr. Paul Tuthill, the voice on subliminal tapes sold by Mind Communications, asserts that nary a shred of evidence suggesting either physical or psychological damage or injury of any kind was offered to a House subcommittee hearing testimony from experts in subliminal communication.

Once again, it is this author's opinion that the final measurement regarding both availability and ethical considerations is and should be consumer based.

The covert application of subliminal technology is another matter, in my opinion. Although there are no documented cases of injury or harm from subliminal programming, the gist of the literature certainly suggests the possibility. The well-known increase in teenage crime accompanied by satanic rituals, symbology, suicide notes, and the like is just one such area of concern. Alas, only an informed and concerned public can help to pass legislation addressing this issue.

Fortunately, the overwhelming majority of researchers and commercial manufacturers openly working with subliminal communication are reliably ethical. There appears to be a sort of "Catch 22" here. If those openly working with subliminals are ethical, then laws are needed to protect us from hidden messages employed by secret producers. How do we discover the messages and pursue the producers? Obviously, herein lies another problem; either everything is policed carefully for subliminals or perhaps paranoia regarding "hidden persuaders" prevails. The issue is complex, but ignoring it will not cause it to go away. Still, if paranoia is where one is at, perhaps some additionally frightening material will provide more pleasure to the panic.

If television is used to project subliminal messages, the Orwellian possibilities are even greater. According to Dick Sutphen, in a transcript from his tape program *The Battle for Your Mind*, Dr. Herbert Krugman has shown that viewers of television demonstrate more right-brain activity than left by a ratio of twofold. For most, using the right brain results in the chemical release of certain natural opiates (encephalins and beta-endorphins). The result is simply that the person feels good. Combine this with the observation of Dr. Thomas Mulholland, a psychophysiologist in Bedford, Massachusetts, who discovered that children's brain-wave patterns are predominantly alpha waves when viewing television, and that the majority of those tested were unable to maintain a predominance of ordinary beta waves even when instructed to concentrate, and the intrigue thickens.

Now, add the dimension of "black slide" or "black frame" technology, whereby every thirty-second frame in a film being projected is blank, thus producing forty-five-beat-per-minute pulsations perceived only at a subconscious level, and we have trance induction. In that case, any suggestion, subliminal or otherwise, is much more likely to be acted upon by the viewer.

While the subject of film speeds is still fresh, it is worth noting that speeding up the standard twenty-four-frame-per-second (FPS) to sixty FPS increases physiological stimulation. In fact, at least one special-effects expert, Douglas Trumball, has tinkered with this concept and refined it to a process he refers to as Showscan. In addition to increasing excitement, Showscan is said to stimulate feelings of voyeurism and facilitate enhanced recall. The possibility of misusing this technology where subliminal input is involved is frightening. On the other hand, utilizing Showscan in an accelerated learning format is exciting.

Still others view subliminal messages as the work of the devil, messing with the mind, un-Christian, and so forth. As a Reverend Doctor, I personally find this perspective both ignorant and unwarranted by the facts.

The mind is influenced by all of life's various stimuli. Life and stimuli are experiences having to do with this physical dimension as at least one significant component. The nature of the physical world is one in which Heraclitus applied the terminology "constant flux." The flux is between energy and matter, as the Einsteinian equation demonstrates. There is no such thing as energy that is inherently evil. Evil is given rise to by the use (or misuse) of energy.

Science has in the past produced technology ranging from the nuclear to the neurosciences. Not all nuclear use is corrupt and destructive nor are our neurosurgeons physicians of a Frankensteinian mentality.

Subliminal communication has as many positive possibilities as applications for subversive use. It is not the technology but the people behind its application that should be examined for motive and intent—good or evil.

I am aware of one Christian group that is considering subliminal audio tapes as a potential proselyter. To any conscientious observer concerned with individual rights, freedom of religion, or the integrity of America's great declaration known as the Bill of Rights, this is as alarming as heavy-metal satanic messages.

Another interesting question that presently is the focus of much research is the nature of the subliminal voice track presented. Should the voice track be multitracked, multifrequencied, sped up as is the process in what is known as time compression, or said slowly, methodically, with contextual reference?

Some manufacturers, as mentioned earlier, are apparently of a "more is better" mentality. I have heard claims that at least one manufacturer produced sixty-minute cassette subliminal recordings with over a million affirmations on each. This same company claims that to copy one of its programs is to lose the subliminal input due to their unique recording process. I was also told by a knowledgeable sound engineer that the method used was not digital and therefore the applied state of the art this company used turned out a product that, if copied, would be as effective as the purchased program from which the copy was made.

In my opinion there are some absolutely outrageous claims surfacing by sellers in competition with other sellers for consumer dollars. With sufficient propaganda, some companies are selling products comparable to those made by others less inclined to aggressive marketing and exaggeration for three to four times the competitor's retail price.

In order to get a million affirmations on a tape sixty minutes long, the affirmations must be multitracked and time compressed. When the human voice is sped up to fifteen and even more times the natural speed of delivery, it is questionable whether the communication resulting is any more meaningful than electromagnetic smog.

If one remembers the Chipmunks for a minute, it is easy to construct some sort of neutral image of what goes on in time compression. Speeding the human voice up from two to three times will produce the Chipmunk sound. It is difficult to imagine the Chipmunks saying anything that is taken seriously, but now speed that up five to seven more times, and the conscious mind simply observes noise.

Dr. Steven Halpern states that the United States government is presently looking into evidence that links sound pollution to physiological dysfunction and electromagnetic smog to molecular mutations. Halpern, an authority on sound and music as it affects the human condition, further suggests that unheard sounds, vibrations, are perhaps as important to our environment as any of those perceived. Maybe this is stretching just a little bit my concern regarding subaudible messages time compressed and multitracked and perhaps even multi-frequencied.

Still, there is another and yet more credible concern. Simply stated, if the conscious mind could make zero sense out of messages audibly presented at such speeds, what on earth leads one to believe that the subconscious could?

Science is well aware that the subconscious perceives many more times the stimuli than that which is available to conscious awareness. However, there exists no scientific proof that the subconscious makes meaningful recordings out of any input that is unintelligible. In fact, the overwhelming consensus of opinion from both professionals and the literature suggests that a subliminal verbal communication should be delivered slowly and methodically.

Recall the Budzynski double blind and the Utah State Prison double blind reported in the last chapter; both studies used real-time verbal subliminals.

Dr. Betty Randolph of Success Center is emphatic about "sink time." Betty told this author that all of her tapes are recorded allowing fifteen-second "sinks" in the subliminal audio track.

In a recent conversation with Dick Sutphen, he stated that

he had just written an article for publication effectively asserting that fifteen-to-one time compression was no more meaningful to the subconscious mind than the whine the conscious mind would hear if the messages were played without the subliminal masking.

This author is ignorant of any study that suggests a spoken verbalization can have any effect if sped up fifteen times and delivered subliminally or otherwise. This would be no more meaningful than a Chinese subliminal to an English-speaking person.

Language is contextual, full of inference and expression values. One can use profanity in a demeanor that is humorous or inciteful. The method of delivery very often implies the meaning. Subliminal verbalizations, in this author's opinion, should be be intoned seriously, spoken slowly and meaningfully, and if multitracked, done so in a sequential "round-robin" manner.

Backward-masking could have its advantages and its disadvantages, or it could be no better or worse than forward speech. If the contextual nature of language is found to be a critical factor in future subliminal research, I suspect the backward approach will be of less value, unless applied to certain very specific resistance factors arising in individual pathologies. This would make an interesting study.

The subconscious mind is not concerned with sentences. A process known as subconscious cerebration takes place when words are put into the subconscious mind. Like a dice tumbler in Las Vegas, the subconscious just sort of tumbles words around. As such, words become separated from each other in their original sentence structure. For this reason, it is absolutely critical that affirmations used in subliminal communication are all positively directed at the focus of change designed to be brought about. For example, a tapering-off smoking script that said, "I find ten cigarettes a day more than enough for me," may tumble around and become "more than ten cigarettes."

It is also important that *no* aversive approaches be included. Since a known deterioration effect to the subliminal may follow its suspended use and the result may be that the nonsmoker starts smoking again, it is irresponsible to leave associations with black lungs and smoking in the subconscious for this creates a psychological predisposition or expectation of lung disease.

Aversive therapy was by and large abandoned a decade ago, due in large part to this type of backlash. Not unlike the iotrogenic effect physicians are careful of, affirmations linking negative sets to the stated objective may bring the negative results into manifestation more than the desired positive. Subliminal verbalizations should also be first person, such as "I this" and "I that."

It is an extremely controversial subject as to whether or not the subconscious accepts negative input, such as "I don't smoke." Therefore, affirmations that are forward positive statements, such as "I breathe deeply," are generally preferred. However, one company manufacturing subliminal tapes, Image Dynamics, couples statements such as "I breathe deeply," "I don't smoke," "I exercise," "I don't smoke," "I am relaxed," "I don't smoke." This company has experienced great success with this program.

Once again, an additional suggestion for directed study emerges. From this author's own experience, every answer produces a handful of new questions.

Since the verbal content of subliminals offered in the marketplace are of such great importance, I lean to the companies that disclose their content. With the exception of the symbiotic fantasy, there is no evidence to indicate advantage in "unknown" content over consciously reviewed content. Remember that the inmates participating in the Utah State Prison study reviewed consciously the entire script, including the symbiotic fantasy.

Perhaps an unwritten expectation should be assumed here. It would seem appropriate for a consumer to expect a subliminal to contain the two symbiotic phrases:

1. Mommy and I are one.
2. It's okay to do better than daddy.

It seems equally rational that a manufacturer would omit these two affirmations from their list of verbal statements. Perhaps in this way the best of both worlds could be achieved.

Another concern regarding verbalizations has nothing to do with the script, but rather with the sex of the voice communicating subliminally. Some research indicates that certain personality types will respond to one or the other (male or female) in a preferential manner.

Dr. Tom Budzynski indicated in a telephone conversation that certain feminist types had experienced reverse effects to his weight-loss program. That is to say, they went on an eating binge for a few days, but the effects were never lasting, other than the women involved ceased using their subliminal tapes. Tom attributes this to the male voice and the strong authoritarian resentment held by certain female subjects for males.

It seems obvious that if a consumer has a problem with a particular self-help title, perhaps they should investigate the voice behind the audible and try a voice of the opposite sex before abandoning the technology. We may well see in the future sex-voice alternatives as a regular part of the commercial menu.

Dr. Betty Randolph, creator of the Success Center tapes, uses both male and female voices on most of her titles. Audio Activation offers a choice of male or female voice for each of their programs. All other companies I am aware of use one or the other.

Another consideration comes from what is known as the dichotic. Over fifteen years ago, Dr. Thomas Budzynski invented an audio muscle-relaxation biofeedback instrument that became the prototype for instruments that followed. Over ten years ago, Tom created an audio cassette relaxation program that is used extensively by professionals today. *Psychology Today* featured Tom's work and findings on the subject of brain lateralization in 1977.

For nearly ten years Dr. Budzynski has incorporated a combination of Twilight Learning (brain biofeedback) with nondirective hypnosis in therapeutic settings. Tom combined this learning with findings from his work in brain lateralization, in particular hemisphere dominance, to create in stereo a different subliminal message to each hemisphere.

In literature distributed by Bob Kahl of Futurehealth, distributors for Budzynski's tapes, three types of subliminal products are available: the standard subliminal version, a hypnotic subliminal, and a dichotic stress response programming. The latter is described as presenting numbers one is supposed to repeat out loud, which thereby distracts the dominant or major hemisphere so the minor will receive the input free of censorship or argument.

It is generally held that for most right-handers, the major hemisphere is the "left brain" and the minor the "right brain." The left brain, then, is usually the discriminate brain; the right brain is the indiscriminate. The left is the analytical, the right is the creative, and so forth. It is also generally accepted that the minor hemisphere processes more deeply emotional content and is the repository for unconscious motives behind habits, beliefs, and attitudes.

Dr. Budzynski's hypnotic subliminals incorporate permissive language such as "It's okay to feel good," directed at the dominant hemisphere, and more authoritarian statements such as "I do feel good," directed at the minor hemisphere. This lateralization delivery is accomplished via earphones. In the instance of the typical right-hander, the permissive and audible message enters the right ear to travel to the left brain while the authoritarian subliminal travels from the left ear to the right brain.

Another company distributing a dichotic product is Success World. One side of their program is subliminal to music and the other side contains a hypnotic subliminal delivered by Dr. Paul Illig.

Research is nonexistent to demonstrate proven dichotic preference. Nevertheless, a highly analytical person may want to try this approach if headphones and time-out for hypnosis are practical.

Still another area to be considered from both researcher and consumer perspective is the primary carrier of the subliminal (e.g., music, nature sounds, etc.). Much new research has recently confirmed the age-old adage that "music calms the savage beast," at least certain types of music.

Dr. Steven Halpern is one of the leaders in a field often referred to as "new age" music. Halpern's music has been field-tested and demonstrated to relieve anxiety and tension levels, increase learning skills, raise pain thresholds, and more. In his book *Sound Health*, Halpern asserts that music is routinely used in the Soviet Union to increase pain thresholds and thereby minimize the use of pharmacology.

One of the major differences in "new-age" music as compared with popular music is that the rhythm is not stop-antipestic, simply meaning there is no beginning, middle, or end. A person can listen to this music over and over and still be unable to hum along or anticipate the movement.

Another leading musician in this area is Jim Oliver. Jim has worked with medical professionals for years measuring major/minor muscle groupings and their responses to different notes, wave frequency formats (e.g., square wave, line wave, etc.), duration of intonation, and so forth. In a telephone conversation, Jim reported work with health professionals that was absolutely astounding. (A paper on their findings is anticipated in the near future.) Jim refers to the study of music regarding psychological and physiological responses as symphonics.

Shiela Ostrander and Lynn Schroeder, authors of *Superlearning*, a must on anyone's reading list, document the use of baroque music as an essential aspect of the superlearning process. They go to great lengths listing various classical pieces that produce the desired effects.

Baroque music, usually largo, seems to give rise to mind entrainment, thereby slowing down brain-wave patterns. This slowing down enhances the learning process for reasons that are not the scope of this work. Combine this with timed repetition of material and incredible increases in learning take place.

Repetitively poised material delivered in this manner is reminiscent of the therapeutic use of the repetition of suggestions often used in hypnosis. For that matter, the same sort of repetition takes place in the media. As Dr. Roy Udolf points out, the repetition of a message with perhaps a slight change like an omission of the concluding portion of an often-viewed ad is especially effective. Perhaps one reason for the effectiveness is the "zeigarnik" effect, which is produced by the omission of the closure expected by the audience.

Advertisers and the entertainment industry have long appreciated the effect music has on the viewer. Among other things, music can excite us, motivate us, raise deep emotion, and build terror.

According to Manfred Clynes, studies clearly suggest that there exist basic neurological forms or patterns that correspond to emotional sets. Clynes refers to this correspondence theory as "essentic forms." Using a computer to play standard notes directly proportional to the intensity and duration associated with different emotions, Clynes discovered that listeners experienced the emotion.

Perhaps some clarification is justified regarding Clynes's method. Clynes originally observed and recorded finger pressure applied by volunteers to pressure-sensitive instrumentation. The participants were asked to express emotions of differing nature in this manner. The conclusion Clynes drew was that the "touch" of music is more emotionally meaningful than the rhythm or pitch.

Drawing on this research, Clynes began to look carefully at the "shape" of emotions, or "sentics." He found that only minimal variations, as slight as 2 percent in the duration or amplitude of notes, were critical as to whether a musical piece was perceived as extremely moving or routine.

Not only do we feel music but with the aid of technology we can examine visual representations. "Cymatic" studies evidence in natural geometry the amazing truth that inorganic matter vibrated by sound produces organic patterns.

Three companies manufacturing audio subliminals match the subliminal script with music designed to specifically enhance the desired objective (i.e., memory skills with baroque music, and so forth).

Superlearning, a company created by Ostrander and Schroeder, Halpern Sound, and Image Dynamics, using the music of Jim Oliver, select certain music tracks to accompany and increase the efficacy of their individual titles. Usually, subliminals created in this manner are the more expensive ones, except for those sold by multilevel organizations feeding entire down lines.

Two other companies offer a music selection for each of their titles, and although the music is not necessarily selected to enhance the subliminal property, it nevertheless provides variety. Based on consumer observation that shows the usual consumer begins with between one and three titles and literally builds a library, music selection becomes important.

The Institute of Human Development and Mind Communications offers music selections ranging from blue grass country to mellow rock.

Although it is possible to enhance one with the other, it is the subliminal, not the music, that is at work in these programs. In fact, Dr. Steven Halpern reported conducting an experiment on just this. He recorded a sleep and a wakefulness tape with identical music. Those who listened to the programs responded according to their content, or as the titles suggest, and one group became sleepy while the other stayed awake.

Music plays a significant role in psychophysical response— stimulating or relaxing, enhancing learning, evoking base emotions, producing balance or discordance, and a compendium of other reactions.

Different beats will produce different results. Advertisers learned that seventy-two beats per minute increase suggestability. Key suggests that seventy-two beats per minute voice, drumbeat, and music appear to suggest one right into the symptoms a product is portended to cure (e.g., headache).

New-age music is usually created with a pantanic scale. Superlearning music formats are almost always in largo.

A large body of classical music lends itself naturally to the production of certain effects in the human animal. According to one French researcher, Mozart pieces played frequently improve health. Mme. Belanger asserts that breathing, cardiovascular, and brain-wave rhythms are coordinated, acting on the unconscious to stimulate perception and receptivity.

Steven Cooter, educational theorist, has monitored his own brain-wave patterns via EEG instrumentation while listening to baroque rhythms. At sixty beats per minute, Cooter discovered a complete and balanced pattern emerged; that is, proportionally balanced beta, alpha, and theta waves were displayed.

Baroque music, usually by Vivaldi, Bach, Handel, Telemann, and Corelli, are integral aspects of superlearning or accelerated learning programs.

At least one manufacturer of tapes containing subliminal messages takes this business about music so seriously that all recordings are real-time recordings. Rapid recording techniques invariably result in the loss of certain high and low frequency ranges. Image Dynamics produces tapes at real-time rates to eliminate this kind of generation loss.

Through the efforts of Dr. Hans Jenny, wave patterns generated by music and sound can be visually displayed. Jenny, working largely from the findings of physicist Ernest Ehladni, discovered that by using liquids, powders, and metal filings scattered on a disc, the geometric patterns displayed by the movement of material caused by the disc resonating in certain areas to notes became more than geometry ordered by mathematics. The new patterns took on the same assemblage as organic shapes. Jenny calls this work "cymatics."

Using a tonoscope, a device that converts sounds issued into a microphone into their corresponding visual configurations, some interesting representations become perceivable. For example, the concluding chord of the *Messiah* by Handel produces a perfect pentagram, or five-pointed star. The mantra "ohm" displays a circle in which triangles form.

In summary, sound definitely shapes responses—responses that can have considerable effect on the human condition.

One interesting observation I have made from the thousands of users that visit our stores is that there almost seems to exist a certain kind of condition-response learning that arises from the association of the music used to carry the subliminal. For example, a person that has used a title (perhaps a stress-free title) responds immediately to the sound of the music for some time after the discontinuance of repeated use. This would make an interesting study and has some inherent ramifications that are somewhat disquieting.

Another form of music is nature's symphony. Something about the gentle sounds of ocean waves or a creek babbling in the background, with occasional bird sounds interspersed, produces a quieting, relaxed atmosphere. Some have asserted that the water sounds appeal to deeply rooted intrauterine experiences, implying that the sound is reminiscent of an earlier sanctuary in the womb. And perhaps this is especially appealing to the child in all of us, an archetypal communication resulting in the production of secure, warm feelings.

At least two manufacturers apply the use of nature sounds to all of their musical backgrounds. One of those companies, Image Dynamics, with which I have direct involvement, feels strongly about the use of nature's various symphonies. Some of their programs even include the rushing sound of wind, as does much of Jim Oliver's music.

There are some other general areas where many questions remain to be answered. In the interest of brevity, there are just three more major concerns that I will deal with in this chapter. They are:

1. Resistances
2. Contraindications
3. Technical engineering possibilities

As was alluded to earlier, there are several possible reasons for resistance patterns that emerge in the use of subliminals. They are as diverse as the sex of the voice to the unknown content of the script. Generally, where the "unknown" is concerned, simply reviewing consciously the verbalization will either surface the anxiety attachment or assuage the Orwellian paranoia. A voice resistance is overcome by simply changing the sex of the voice. But there can be many other complex reasons for resistance, and although this occurs rarely, nevertheless I am of the opinion that use should be discontinued if the resistance persists for more than twenty repetitions of the title.

Most resistances are simply feelings of discomfort and are resolved with repeated usage of the subliminal. However, and although I have never heard of this, should some frightful result be encountered, I would suggest not only cessation of the use but consultation with an appropriate professional.

Subliminals are *not* a replacement for professional health care, and although many professionals use them, their use is to facilitate or augment beneficial gains in an ancillary way.

Subliminals are not quick fixes, but their use is doubly appealing, principally because they are extremely affordable and require very little effort to use or to produce the gains desired.

A more common resistance often encountered is one that is tied to choices. All behavior is the result of choices—some consciously adopted, but for the most part made at an unconscious level. I remember using a stop-smoking subliminal. After about ten days, it occurred to me one morning that my cigarettes tasted nasty and, what was worse, the smell was nauseating. Instead of stopping smoking, I *chose* to stop playing the subliminal cassette.

Dr. Budzynski related a somewhat comparable story in a phone conversation. He recalled using a subliminal experiment that contained an aversive verbalization. The subliminal might make one sick but it did not stop the smoking.

So far as contraindications are concerned, it is generally accepted that individuals with serious maladaptive pathologies should be under professional care. Use of a subliminal in this setting is entirely dependent upon the health care professional.

Literature dealing with subliminals and schizophrenics suggest controversial findings. One patient of an associate of Budzynski's reported relief as a result of using a subliminal. However, the relief, together with an unwillingness to play the tape, sharply ended when the patient was shown the subliminal script (it included a symbiotic fantasy) at the patient's insistence. Dr. Budzynski told me that this was not an unexpected outcome, given the history of this patient.

All in all, however, there is absolutely no documented evidence of subliminal self-help programs producing harm. Even the old symptom substitution argument does not apply. As Ostrander and Schroeder document in their *Subliminal Report*, where subliminals are concerned, one need not experience a restriction in one area due to a gain in another.

Positive suggestion is as old as history itself. The principle difference where subliminal communication is concerned is that the conscious mind cannot argue and thereby influence or erode the efficacy of the suggestion's content. It is as simple as a scenario whereby one is told that he feels great and he responds, as we all might, with "Well, maybe" or "No, I don't." The positive suggestion has been filtered, influenced, and interpreted by the cognitive process.

More than perhaps in any part of recent history, the words "you are what you think you are" echo with new meaning. Subliminal communication can facilitate the "think" to accommodate the "think" that one desires, not the "think" that is laden with self-doubt and limitation.

The last area to be discussed in this chapter relevant to unanswered questions deals with technical aspects of production. Since this work is not intended to be a sound engineer's supplement, I will be extremely brief. First, if digital recording is employed, what clock rates or vibrating frequencies are preferred as carriers for subliminal scripts? Second, is digital preferred to analog? Third, at what decible threshold does communication perceived at a subliminal level cease to be perceivable?

In the years to come I am certain that most, if not all, of these areas will be fully investigated.

One last, although I am hesitant to mention it, area of research that I personally am interested in is one of intentionality.

Our quantum physicists inform us that everything ultimately is wave form in a sea of electromagnetic energy. One new vista of discovery, that referred to as the "M-field Theory," further suggests that not only is there a connective circle between thought and wave form but that thought can and is influenced by some interaction occurring at an unseen level—wave form.

The "M-field Theory" is suggested by evidence that testifies to the fact that learning a subject, any subject—Morse Code, for example—occurs more rapidly when the subject matter has been previously learned by other groups or individuals. The more learning that has occurred or taken place with a subject, the easier it is for a new individual or group to learn. It is directly proportional, one to the other. Jung's collective unconscious revisited?

It is my opinion that electromagnetic processes, including the simple ones involved in manufacturing cassette tapes, magnetic encoding of sound-wave transmissions, are equally subject to thought transmissions. In other words, I believe that "intentionality" could influence the subliminal efficacy of any experiment. The question this author has is a simple one. Could intentionality alone be perceived and acted upon via the modality of subliminal input? I think so. It would make for an interesting experiment, to say the least. I am aware of one subliminal manufacturer that blesses their master recordings just as the cleric blesses holy water.

Finally, there are some frequently asked consumer-related questions about self-help subliminals. In a one, two, three fashion I will relate the question and the answer.

Question: Can more than one program be used at a time without disadvantage?

Answer: Yes, provided that no two programs undertake major behavioral modification. For example, one would not want to attempt cessation of drug abuse and weight loss at the same time. Most of the literature suggests that compatible titles such as memory improvement and good study habits would enhance one another. Using unrelated titles that are non-threatening to one's basic drive mechanisms, such as removal of warts and taking examinations, is just as efficient as using only one.

Question: How often should the tapes be used?

Answer: You literally *cannot* overdose on positive suggestions. Many users have reported incredible results where automatic reverse players have been employed to continuously expose them for several days to a subliminal program. Nearly all manufacturers guarantee their products on the basis of recommended usage that consists of listening to the program once a day for thirty days.

Question: Is there a best time to listen to the tapes?

Answer: One can use the tapes as background while involved in any activity. No deliberate listening intensity is required. Users have reported excellent results utilizing subliminal programs at bedtime, during drive times, and even while watching television. Again, no conscious effort is involved.

Question: How do I know that what I'm getting is actually the message they say is on the tape?

Answer: By purchasing from major manufacturers that disclose their subliminal content, the old law of the dollar rules. To chance an entire profitable business by covertly "messing" with the stated scripts simply does not make any sense. It is easy with the right technology to "take apart" and examine the content on most tapes.

Question: How soon can I expect results from using a subliminal tape?

Answer: Most people sense beneficial results within a week or two. All should be aware of gains within sixty days if the program is solidly conceived and produced.

Question: Who uses subliminal programs?

Answer: Everyone from health professionals to educators. Many athletic programs, sales organizations, government agencies, retailers, and others use subliminals, to say nothing of the millions of individual users.

CHAPTER 9

THE "HOMEMADE" SUBLIMINAL

Creating an audio cassette subliminal that works is a relatively simple process, although perhaps too expensive to prove practical.

The procedure outlined in this chapter was used by the author in his early research. In fact, it was this process that was used to create the subliminal titled "A Gift of Love" that is used by the Sunrise people (a support group for survivors of suicide victims) in Utah. Testimonial evidence suggests that it works very well.

There are six steps involved, including the acquisition of equipment. This process will *not* produce commercial quality from the standpoint of professional audio mastering, but will provide a usable product.

There are certain advantages to creating your own subliminal property. One should weigh the advantages against the professional quality standard before investing the time or money necessary to produce a personalized subliminal program.

Some of the obvious advantages include:

1. The subliminal script is uniquely and precisely what a person desires. (Be careful here—much bad karma will come from deliberate or exploitive misuse.)

2. The music or principle sound carrier is personally chosen and thereby affords a broader selection based on preferences. One may choose the gentle sounds of a waterfall or ocean waves as the only principle carrier because the use will be as background while viewing television.

I am reminded here of a woman who played surreptitiously to her teenagers a good study habits program produced by Success Center and carried by ocean waves while they viewed television. She reported that within a short time the teenagers turned off the television set and moved to their rooms to study.

Whatever the primary carrier, be careful of copyright infringements!

3. The voice on the subliminal track can be your own. There is much research suggesting that one responds advantageously to his or her own voice in many circumstances.

The steps to creating a custom program are:
1. Select and obtain the equipment.
2. Write and record the script.
3. Record the white sound.
4. Mix the script recording with white sound.
5. Select the principle carrier.
6. Mix the product of "step 3" with the principle carrier.

Equipment Selection

The equipment needed consists of three cassette players, one of which must have recording and external input capability and the other two must be equipped with external output functions, a two- to four-channel sound mixer, and a white-sound generator. Inexpensive mixers are readily available from places like Radio Shack.

White-sound units are available from a number of variety and hardware outlets including Sears, Roebuck & Co. This is a simple and relatively inexpensive device that generates the sounds of running water, ocean surf, etc. A person will also need at least four blank cassettes of the chosen length.

Subliminal Scripting

Write your affirmations in an all positive manner (see Chapter 8), then speak them slowly and meaningfully into a recorder. Repeat the script over and over for the desired length of time. When through, rewind the audio track now containing the verbalization.

White-Sound Recording

Now record another cassette with the chosen white sound, possibly ocean waves. This recording should be the same length as the audio-voice track; for example, thirty minutes.

First Mix

Using the players with external output, connect the mixer (mono: two channels; stereo: four channels). Adjust the mixing volume such that one can barely perceive the spoken affirmations when mixed with the ocean sound. When all adjustments are made, record the mix using the recorder with external input for the desired length of the finished product.

The Principle Carrier

Select now the principle carrier. For our homemade version, music generally works best, although one can remix white sound with white sound. Place this tape, and if not a tape, convert it to a cassette tape, in the player that had carried the voice recording.

Finale

Place the recorded product of your first mix in the player that formerly carried the white-sound-only recording and mix your two recordings onto one new master.

Good luck and remember the Golden Rule!

As a footnote, you may want to inquire of one of the established companies distributing subliminal products, before going to the time and expense involved in creating your own. Many companies will provide custom subliminal work for substantially less than the cost of equipment to produce homemade tapes.

CHAPTER 10

IN SUMMARY

Anyone that takes the time and effort necessary to review the literature, conduct studies, and otherwise become fully involved at an interactive level with a subject is deserving of an opinion on that subject.

Subliminal communication transcends boundaries inherent to disciplines. There is no specialized discipline graduating students with degrees in "subliminal."

Opinions are always relative to the contextual reference implied by "authority." I do not hold myself out to be an authority, but I do maintain I have a right to an opinion. I am not sure that there is any such thing as an authority on subliminal communication, even though there exist some very good authorities on various aspects of it.

Subliminal communication for the most part is still in the investigative stages. Because this is true, most of those working with subliminal this and subliminal that view themselves as pioneers.

By way of recapitulation, and in this pioneer's opinion, subliminal communication is one of the most promising means by which to explore dynamically the pragmatic power of the mind.

In the metaphor of Maxwell Maltz, many of us have become slaves to our unconscious computers. Our synthetic experiences are generally negative, our expectations are almost invariably limiting; this biocomputer, functioning as a servo-auto-mechanism, is programming dismal realities despite our conscious kicking and struggling—perhaps because most of us were raised that way; raised to believe we couldn't, wouldn't, and shouldn't—shouldn't even try for the most part. Like any calculator when it is asked to compute, if there is more negative input than positive, the result is negative.

Subliminal offers an affordable and effortless way to rewrite and rebalance the language and equations existing in the biocomputer, the unconscious or subconscious mind. Thus, we really have an opportunity to truly assume charge of the controls. We can indeed change ourselves and the world around us. With this realization the possibilities become limitless.

Today you can be what you think you are, not what others thought you might be. You can indeed become the product of your own creation—not the projection viewed from the lenses of others.

You are indeed self-responsible! As my dear friend, Professor William Guillory, puts it in his wonderful book *Realizations*: "Personal empowerment comes through self-awareness."

APPENDIX A

THURSTONE MEASUREMENT TABLE

(A)   Activity

(V)   Vigorousness

(I)   Impulsiveness

(D)   Dominance

(E)   Stability

(S)   Sociability

(R)   Reflectivity

ADULT PROFILE

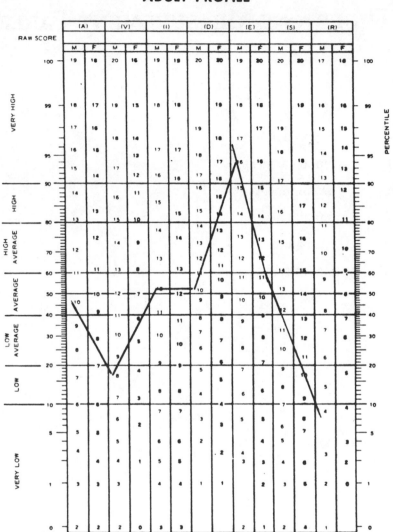

Figure 1. Pre-test measurement.

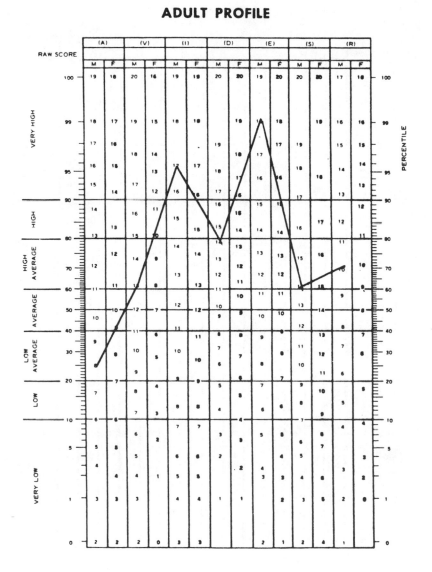

Figure 2. Post-test measurement.

ADULT PROFILE

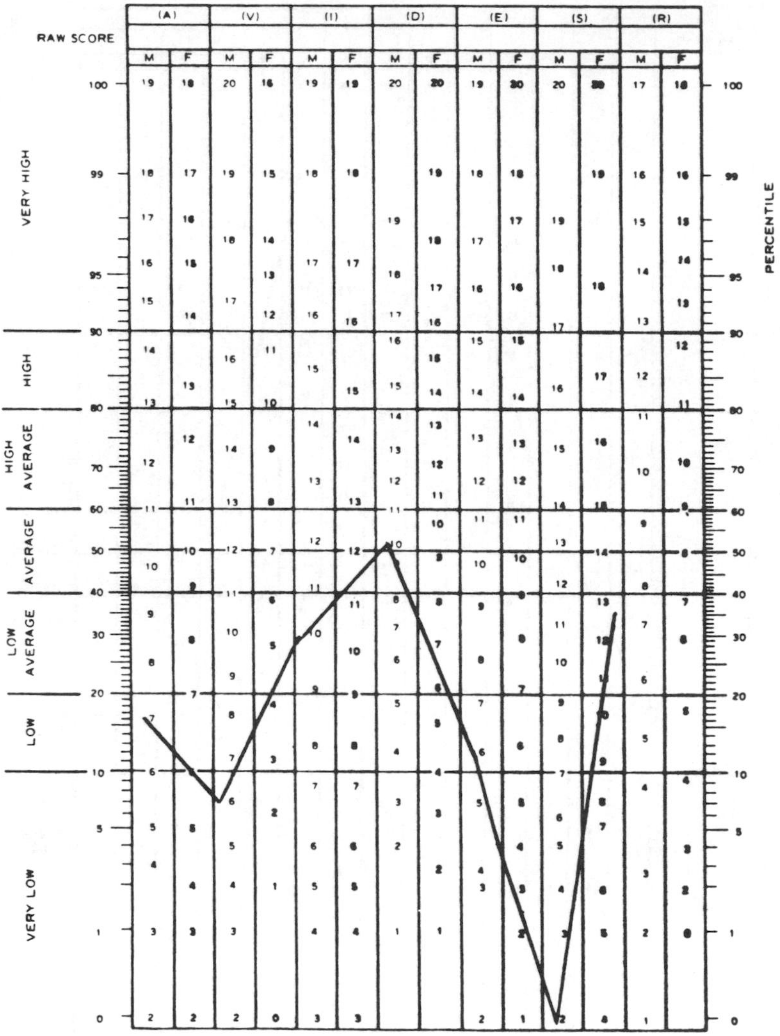

Figure 3.   Pre-test measurement.

ADULT PROFILE

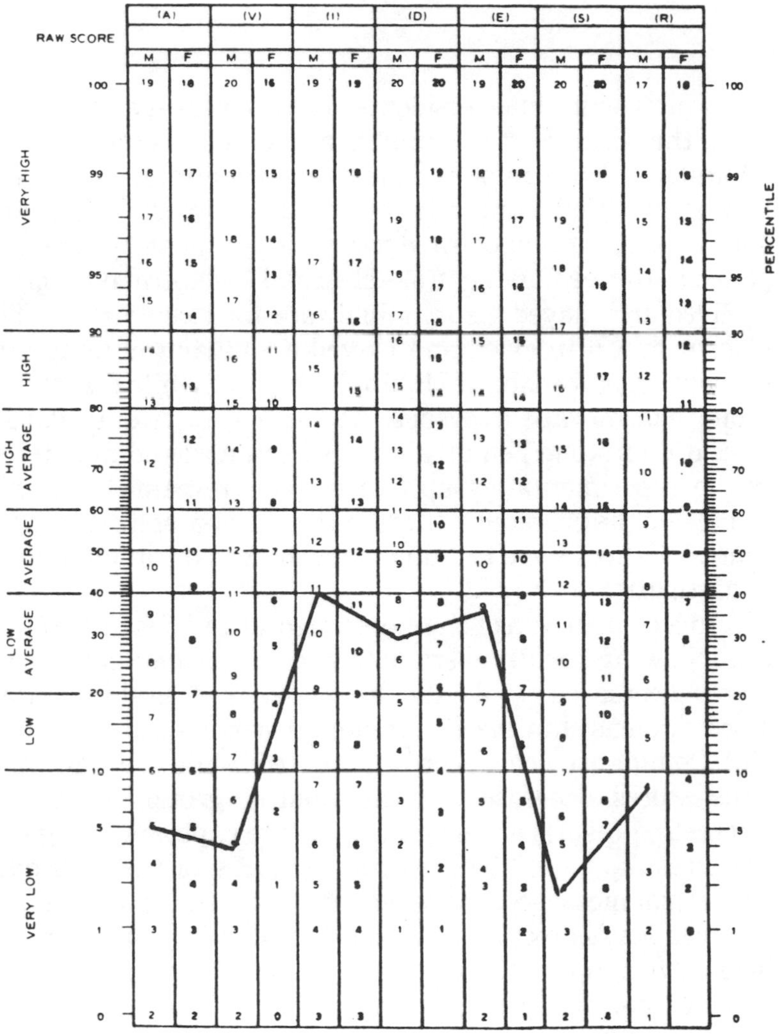

Figure 4. Post-test measurement.

APPENDIX B

ABSTRACT

Thirty-eight male residents (average age—twenty three) from the Unit at the Utah State Prison completed the Thurstone Temperament Schedule in a voluntary participatory study. Following administration, subjects were randomly placed into one of three groups (experimental—fourteen, placebo—thirteen, and control—eleven). The experimental group received and played a subliminal tape for twenty days. The placebo group received and played a similar sounding tape without an embedded subliminal message, while the control group had no tape exposure. At the end of twenty days a second Thurstone Temperament Schedule was administered. In the experimental group five subjects remained who had completed the procedure, three in the placebo, and eight in the control. Others were lost due to discharges or unwillingness to participate.

In a comparison of the experimental and control groups, the following results were obtained. The Dominance scale scores decreased while the Reflective and Stability scale scores increased in the Experimental group (desired effects). The Dominance scale scores increased while the Reflective scale scores decreased in the Control group. These are interesting results across groups. In the experimental group these results would be predicted by focus of the embedded subliminal messages. In the placebo group the opposite effect obtained may be explained by the fact that they (the subjects) listened to a tape without a message and felt no change. They obtained no reinforcement to continue, and possibly experienced some frustration.

It is stressed that this pilot study had limitations, especially time of implementation and sample size.

It is not the intention of the experimenters to generalize beyond the obtained results. However, it must be stressed that to evaluate an incarcerated population was a very unique opportunity; to our knowledge this was the first time subliminal technology has been evaluated with this population. The results indicated change and strongly suggest the need for further research with benefit to these individuals and society in general, as this technology is better understood and applied in a wide variety of applications and settings.

Experimental			Control		
Predifferences to postdifferences			Predifferences to postdifferences		
Scale Movement	Variable	Rate of Change	Scale Movement	Variable	Rate of Change
↑	Stability	+3.4	↑	Stability	+ .8
↑	Reflectivity	+2.6	↓	Reflectivity	-1.0
↓	Dominance	-2.7	↑	Dominance	+1.4

Figure 5. Comparisons between the experimental group and the control group.

APPENDIX D

SUBLIMINAL SUPPLIER LIST

Advanced Learning Systems, Inc.
7131 Owensmouth Ave.
Canoga Park, CA 91303

Audio Activation, Inc.
10 Waterside Plaza, Ste. 14A
New York, NY 10010

Earth Education
P.O. Box 747
Fairfield, IA 52556

Effective Learning Systems, Inc.
5221 Edina Ind. Blvd.
Edina, MN 55435

Futurehealth, Inc.
975 A Bristol Pike
Bensalem, PA 19020

Gateways Research Institute
P.O. Box 41
Ojai, CA 93023

Steven Halpern
260 W. Broadway
New York, NY 10013

Hypnovision Video
25 Drydan Lane
Providence, RI 02904

Image Dynamics
557 California Street
Suite 118
Boulder City, NV 89005

Institute of Human Development
Box 1616
Ojai, CA 93023

Institute of Noetic Metaphysics
Drawer 7116
S.L.C., UT 84107

John-David Learning Institute
2740 Roosevelt St.
Carlsbad, CA 92008

Light Unlimited
Box 8062
Durango, CO 81301

Midwest Research
6515 Highland Rd. #203
Pontiac, MI 48054

Mind Communications
945 Burton SW
Grand Rapids, MI 49509

Mind Mint
4150 South 1785 West
Carriage Square Plaza
S.L.C., UT 84119

Mystic Trader
Box 2496
Coeur d'Alene, ID 83814

Potentials Unlimited
4808 Broodmore
Grand Rapids, MI 49508

Power Learning
22704 Ventura Blvd.
Woodland Hills, CA 91364

Psychodynamics
3202 W. Anderson Lane #203
Austin, TX 78757

Psycho Synergetics Inc.
PSI Power Programs
Box 60415
Las Vegas, NV 89160-0415

Success Education Institute
Box 90608
San Diego, CA 92109-3602

Success World
83 King St., Suite 220
Seattle, WA 98104

Superlearning
450 Seventh Ave.
New York, NY 10123

Valley of the Sun
Box 2010
Malibu, CA 90265

Warner Audio
Box 211
New York, NY 10011

SELECTED BIBLIOGRAPHY

Adams, V. (1982, May). "Mommy and I are one": Beaming messages to inner space. *Psychology Today, 16*(9), 24.

Arima, S., & Sillar, J. (1982). Effects of subliminal oneness stimuli in Hebrew on academic performance of Israeli high school students: Further evidence on the adaptation-enhancing effects of symbiotic fantasies in another culture using another language. *Journal of Abnormal Psychology, 91*(5).

Baker, L. E. (1937). The influence of subliminal stimuli upon verbal behavior. *Journal of Experimental Psychology, 20.*

Becker, H. C., Chamberlain, S., Burt, S., Heisse, J., & Marino, D. Poster session reported to the American Society of Clinical Hypnosis, 25th Annual Scientific Meeting.

Becker, H. C., & Charbonnet, K. D. (1980, March 28). *Applications of Subliminal Video and Audio Stimuli in Therapeutic, Educational, Industrial, and Commercial Settings.* Eighth Annual Northeast Bioengineering Conference, Massachusetts Institute of Technology, Cambridge.

Becker, H. C., Charbonnet, K. D., Warren, E. S. III, Corrigan, R. D., Schmidt, L. F. III, Griffin, C. E. Jr., Penick, R. M. III, & Ryder, F. V. III. (September 30-October 3, 1980). *New Subliminal Processors for Therapy, Industry, and Education.* 33rd Annual Conference on Engineering in Medicine and Biology (ACEMB), Washington, D.C.

Becker, H. C., Corrigan, R. E., Elder, S. T., Tallant, J. D., & Goldstein, M. (1965, August 22-27). Subliminal communication: Biological engineering considerations. In *Digest of the 6th International Conference on Medical Electronics and Biological Engineering* (pp. 452-453). Tokyo, Japan.

Becker, H. C., & Elder, S. T. (1966, September 5-11). Can subliminal perception be useful to the psychiatrist? *Excerpta Medica* (International Congress Series No. 117). Abstract of paper presented to the IV World Congress of Psychiatry, Madrid, Spain.

Becker, H. C., & Glauzer, N. H. (1978, April 10-12). Subliminal communication: Advances in audiovisual engineering applications for behavior therapy and education. *Proceedings of the 1978 Institute of Electrical and Electronics Engineering Region 3 Conference.*

Becker, H. C., Jewell, J. F., & Alito, P. (1977, March 13-17). Video and audio signal monitors/processors for subliminal communication in weight control. *Proceedings of the 12th Annual Meeting of the Association for the Advancement of Medical Instrumentation (AAMI).* San Francisco.

Becker, H. C., & McDonagh, E. W. (1979, November). Subliminal communication (subliminal psychodynamic activation) in rehabilitative and preventive medicine. *Proceedings of the Ninth Annual Conference of the Society for Computer Medicine.* Atlanta.

Bevin, W. (1964, February). Subliminal stimulation: A pervasive problem for psychology. *Psychological Bulletin, 61*(2), 84-92.

Borgeat, F., Chabot, R., & Chaloult, L. (1981). Subliminal perception and level of activation. *Canadian Journal of Psychiatry, 26*(4).

Bower, B. (1978, March 8). Subliminal messages: Changes for the better? *Science News,* 129(3), 156.

Bryant-Tuckett, R., & Silverman, L. H. (1984). Effects of the subliminal stimulation of symbiotic fantasies on the academic performance of emotionally handicapped students. *Journal of Counseling Psychology, 31.*

Budzynski, T. (1977). Tuning in on the Twilight Zone. *Psychology Today, 11*(3), 38-44.

Costello, M. (1986, March). The ultimate brain trip. *Omni Magazine.*

Dauber, R. (1984). Subliminal psychodynamic activation in depression: On the role of autonomy issues in depressed college women. *Journal of Abnormal Psychology, 93*(1).

Dixon, N. F. (1971). *Subliminal Perception: The Nature of a Controversy.* London: McGraw-Hill.

Dixon, N. (1981). *Preconscious Processing.* New York: Wiley.

Dunham, W. R. (1894). *The Science of Vital Force.* Boston: Damrell and Upham.

Eroelyi, M. H. (1974). A new look at the new look: Perceptual defense and vigilance. *Psychological Review, 81,* 1-25.

Ferguson, M. (1985). Brain mind bulletin. *Perspective, 7*(4).

Ferguson, M. (1986). Brain mind bulletin. *Perspective, 11*(9).

Fisher, C. (1956). Dreams, images, and perception: A study of unconscious-preconscious relationships. *Journal of the American Psychoanalytic Association, 4,* 5-48.

Frauman, D. C. et al. (1984). Effect of subliminal symbiotic activation on hypnotic rapport and susceptibility. *Journal of Abnormal Psychology, 93*(4).

Hall, E. (1986, February). *Psychology Today, 20*(6), 46.

Halpern, S. (1985). *Sound Health.* San Francisco: Harper & Row.

Hayden, B., & Silverstein, R. (1983). The effects of tachistoscopic oedipal stimulation on competitive dart throwing. *Psychological Research Bulletin, 23*(1).

Hoban, P. (1984, July). Subliminal software. *Omni, 6*(1), 30.

Kaplan, M. J. (1984, May). The cassette connection: 127 hours and 6 minutes to a new you. *Cosmopolitan, 197*(4), 136.

Key, W. (1974). *Subliminal Seduction.* New York: Signet.

Key, W. (1981). *Clam Plate Orgy.* New York: Signet.

Klaine, J. (1980, July). Subliminal world. *Petersen's Photographic Magazine, 9*(8), 45.

Klein, G. S., Spence, D. P., Holt, R. R., & Gourevitch, S. (1958). Cognition without awareness: Subliminal influences upon conscious thought. *Journal of Abnormal Social Psychology, 54.*

Kramer, J. (1986, September-November). Psychic guide. In *Subliminal Persuasion, Becoming All You Can Be* (pp. 33-36).

Lander, E. (1981, February). In through the out door. *Omni, 3*(6), 44.

Levine, A. (1986, February). The great subliminal self-help hoax. *New Age Magazine.*

Lozanov, G. (1971). *Suggestology.* Sophia: Nauki i Izkustvi.

Lozanov, G. (1978). *Suggestology and Outlines of Suggestopedy.* New York: Gordon & Breach.

Maltz, M. (1960). *Psychocybernetics.* New York: Simon & Schuster.

McGinley, L. (1986, January 1). Uncle Sam believes messages about mom help calm nerves. *Wall Street Journal.*

Molfese, D. (1985, November). When is a word a word? *Psychology Today.*

Moore, T. E. (1985, July). Subliminal delusion. *Psychology Today, 19*(2), 10.

Morse, R. C., & Stoller, D. (1982, September). The hidden message that breaks habits. *Science Digest, 90*(1), 28.

Muse, D. (1984, April). Expando-vision: User-friendly manipulations? *Microcomputing, 8*(2), 64.

Nachmias, D. (1981, March). Subliminal politics. *Annals of American Academic Politics and Social Science, 454*(2), 230.

Ostrander, S., & Schroeder, L. (1980). *Superlearning.* New York: Delta.

Ostrander, S., & Schroeder, L. (1985). *Subliminal Report.* New York: Superlearning.

Packard, V. (1957). *Hidden Persuaders.* New York: Affiliated Publishers.

Packard, V. (1981, February). The new (and still hidden) persuaders. *Reader's Digest, 118*(4), 120.

Palmatier, J. R., & Bornstein, P. H. (1980). Effects of subliminal stimulation of symbiotic merging fantasies on behavioral treatment of smokers. *Journal of Nervous and Mental Disease, 168,* 715-720.

Parker, K. A. (1982). Effects of subliminal symbiotic stimulation on academic performance: Further evidence on the adaptation-enhancing effects of one's fantasies. *Journal of Counseling Psychology, 29,* 19-28.

Romberg, L. (1975). *Workings of Your Mind.* Burlington, Ontario: Audio Cybernetics.

Rose, C. (1985). *Accelerated Learning.* Great Britain.

Sackeim, H., Packer, I. K., & Gur, R. C. (1977). Hemisphericity, cognitive set, and susceptibility to subliminal perception. *Journal of Abnormal Psychology, 86,* 624-630.

Sandler, C. (1985, February 19). Mind altering software: Do you want to trance? *PC, 4*(1), 42.

Schmeidler, G. (1986). Subliminal perception and ESP: Order in diversity? *The Journal of the American Society for Physical Research, 80*(3).

Silverman, L. H. (1979). Two unconscious fantasies as mediators of successful psychotherapy. *Psychotherapy: Theory and Practice, 16,* 215-230.

Silverman, L. H. (1980a). Is subliminal psychodynamic activation in trouble? *Journal of Abnormal Psychology.*

Silverman, L. H (1980b). A comprehensive report of studies using the subliminal psychodynamic activation method. *Psychological Research Bulletin, 20*(3).

Silverman, L. H., & Candell, P. (1970). On the relationship between aggressive activation, symbiotic merging intactness of body boundaries and manifest pathology in schizophrenia. *Journal of Nervous and Mental Disease, 150,* 387-399.

Silverman, L. H., Candell, P., Pettit, T. F., & Blum, F. A. (1971). Further data on effects of aggressive activation and symbiotic merging on ego functioning of schizophrenics. *Perceptual and Motor Skills, 32,* 93-94.

Silverman, L. H., Lachmann, F. M., & Milich, R. H. (1984). Unconscious oneness fantasies: Experimental findings and implications for treatment. *International Forum for Psychoanalysis, 1*(2).

Silverman, L. H., Levinson, P., Mendelsohn, E., Ungaro, R., & Bronstein, A. (1975). A clinical application of subliminal psychodynamic activation: On the stimulation of symbiotic fantasies as an adjunct in the treatment of hospitalized schizophrenics. *Journal of Nervous and Mental Disease, 161,* 379-392.

Silverman, L. H., Martin, A., Ungaro, R., & Mendelsohn, E. (1978). Effect of subliminal stimulation of symbiotic fantasies on behavior modification treatment of obesity. *Journal of Consulting and Clinical Psychology, 46,* 432-441.

Silverman, L. H., Ross, D. L., Adler, J. M., & Lustig, D. A. (1978). Simple research paradigm for demonstrating subliminal dynamic activation: Effects of oedipal stimuli on dart-throwing accuracy in college males. *Journal of Abnormal Psychology, 87.*

Subliminal Tapes, Venture Onward. (1986, July/August).

Sutphen, D. (1982). *Battle for Your Mind* (Transcript from speech delivered to World Congress of Hypnotists). Malibu, CA: Valley of the Sun Publishing.

Thompson, M. E. (1980, September). Technology as a craft of deceit. *USA Today, 109*(4), 16.

Tomlinson, K. (1983, January). Just snore that weight off. *Los Angeles, 28*(2), 206.

Trewin, I. (1984, January 6). Auberon Waugh: Subliminal plagiarism for Lord of the Flies? *Publishers Weekly, 225*(1), 22.

Udolph, R. (1981). *Handbook of Hypnosis for Professionals.*